Kelly,

May the wind
at your back. And the
sun shine bright on your
future. Live the Code.

Blessings

BEATITUDE
CODE

BEATITUDE
CODE

The Art of Living
Perfectly Imperfect Lives

J. Steve Bruner

XULON ELITE

Xulon Press Elite
555 Winderley Pl, Suite 225
Maitland, FL 32751
407.339.4217
www.xulonpress.com

Paperback ISBN-13: 978-1-66289-779-5
Hard Cover ISBN-13: 978-1-66289-780-1
Ebook ISBN-13: 978-1-66289-781-8

TO SHERRY

the music of my life

"Life is not a problem to be solved, but a reality to be experienced."

Søren Kierkegaard

TABLE OF CONTENTS

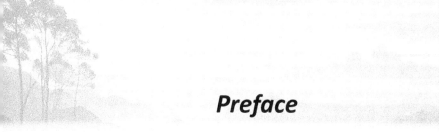

Preface

"The privilege of a lifetime is to become who you truly are."
Carl Gustav Jung

How, Then, Shall We Live?

As the final words of the *Beatitude Code* flowed from my pen, I realized the book was a long-awaited gift I would have enjoyed giving to my younger self. While working hard, raising a family, and trying to live a full life, I developed a passion for exploring Scripture, philosophy, and theology. Within me resided a prophetic voice, compelling me to seek the holy grail of my convictions. I was confident it existed somewhere, and yet, the irony is, I knew my role was to keep looking for it, somehow knowing all along I would never find it, that it would find me, and it did.

Amid the expansive and intricate terrain of theological and philosophical thought, a persistent feeling gnawed at me, a sense that something fundamental and indispensable remained elusive. It was as though the rich mosaic of these intellectual and spiritual traditions, while undeniably extraordinary, left a distinct void in my quest for a deeper understanding and connection to my purpose and beliefs.

Then, like a revelation in plain sight, the Beatitudes—eight paradoxical truths before me all along—suddenly sprang to life. In their wisdom, I discovered the missing piece that ignited the enlightenment of my salvation, and the parts of the puzzle started falling into place.

Philosophers, theologians, and great thinkers throughout history have grappled with several profound questions exploring the essence of human existence, the universe, and the nature of reality. Among these, the questions of existence stand paramount:

- Who am I?
- What is the purpose of life?
- Why should the existence of God hold significance in my life?

Pondering these deep questions takes us beyond the mundane aspects of everyday life. These inquiries prompt us to consider God's existence and how this affects our lives. Such reflections also spark curiosity about the afterlife, the nature of our souls, and paths to attaining greater consciousness and purpose. Ultimately, these contemplations bring us to a pivotal point of decision-making. There are two questions each of us must answer for ourselves. The answer we give to these questions ultimately defines us:

- What are you willing to live for?
- What are you willing to die for?

Preacher's Kid

Growing up, the church was my second home. My father was a minister who instilled in our family the essence of a life dedicated to a higher calling. I was deeply immersed in this environment, yet somehow, I often felt like an outsider within my own story. There I was on the periphery, a part of it all but simultaneously distanced, quietly observing, and selectively sifting through my beliefs, trying to determine which elements resonated with my true self and which didn't.

Washington

As I approached ninth grade, a seismic shift in my life transported us from the tall pine trees and red clay of Georgia to the bustling heart of the nation, Washington, D.C. The abrupt change was nothing short of surreal, thrusting me into the epicenter of power during the tumultuous 1960s.

As I settled into this new world, the air was thick with the winds of change. Civil rights fervor ignited the streets, anti-Vietnam War protests reverberated through the city, and the iconic Lincoln Memorial hosted exhilarating free concerts that seemed to resonate with the very soul of the era. The space race's promise of exploring the cosmos painted the horizon with boundless dreams.

Musical legends like Janis Joplin, Joan Bias, Bob Dylan, The Mamas & the Papas, Jimi Hendrix, ELO, The Beatles, The Rolling Stones, and The Who permeated the airwaves with their electrifying tunes and rebellious spirit. Every weekend, one of the big names of rock 'n' roll played in the D.C. area. None of these things had been part of who I was only a year earlier, but now, they swirled around me, and I was in the middle of it all.

I attended Walt Whitman High School in Bethesda, Maryland, a mosaic of people from every state in America and the world—Jews, Protestants, Catholics, Moslems, Hindus, Buddhists, South Americans, Europeans, Atheists, conservatives, and liberals. Powerful opposing forces were at play, yet beneath the surface; there was a profound sense that everyone was looking to correct wrongs while rediscovering our highest ideas.

Amid all of this, the Cold War between the United States and the Soviet Union cast a shadow of apprehension over the nation. The looming specter of a nuclear conflict weighed heavily on everyone's minds, a constant reminder of the precarious balance of power in those challenging times.

From ninth grade until graduation, I was thrust into a whirlwind of historical significance, where the world was shifting and evolving around me. It was a time of immense change and uncertainty, and I, a participant, was forever marked by the indelible imprints of that extraordinary era.

The Nightmare

Shortly after we arrived in Washington, a recurring nightmare began to haunt my nights. In this vivid dream, the sinister specter of Soviet forces had descended upon the city, ruthlessly seizing control. The invaders, with their cold, unyielding demeanor, had lined up the residents, forcing them to confront an agonizing choice: Renounce their faith in Christ and pledge unwavering allegiance to the Communists, or be shot.

In the nightmare's surreal landscape, a chill gripped my heart as I stood in line. At the far end of the line, a contingent of soldiers, clad in the uniform of the oppressor, posed the ominous question to each trembling soul. "Do you deny Christ and accept Communism?" The air was thick with tension, punctuated by sporadic gunshots that echoed through the anguish-filled atmosphere as people fell to the unforgiving ground.

In the hazy recesses of my dream state, a profound internal struggle unfolded. I contemplated the unthinkable. Could I utter the word "yes" to save my life, all the while harboring a whispered confession to God and myself that I did not truly mean it? I yearned for survival, for the chance to witness the unfolding of the rest of my life, for I was but a tender sixteen-year-old with an insatiable hunger for experiences yet to come.

The enigmatic conclusion forever eluded me as my dream always ended before the soldiers reached my place in line.

I share this with you not merely as a personal story, but because I am convinced that, deep within the recesses of our souls, my dream confronts the fundamental essence of our existence. This nightmare goes beyond being lost in one's sleep. It brings to the surface an innate longing, an insatiable quest to unearth our deepest convictions.

What are we willing to live for and what are we willing to die for that ultimately defines who we are?

Midlife

Fast forward through two decades of a career in the computer industry, and life as I knew it was turned on its head. Amid the throes of clinical depression, I found myself in a dark and challenging place, yet it was in this very abyss that something extraordinary happened. God used one of my greatest struggles, my breakdown, to catalyze an unprecedented breakthrough. This intense turmoil became a transformative journey, reshaping my life, faith, and understanding of everything.

At my lowest point, Yahweh (God, I AM) threw me a lifeline called the Beatitudes, eight paradoxical teachings of Jesus. They were always in plain sight my entire life, and yet it took a spiritual epiphany where the Christ Spirit opened the eyes of my spirit to see something I had missed. I suddenly saw an entire cosmos of truth interconnected in a kaleidoscope of awe and wonder, and everything I had been looking for—culture, Scripture, history, and my life—suddenly made sense.

I always thought finding what I was searching for would be like a scene from a movie when the hero discovers a secret clue in a mysterious cave or on an old, dusty library shelf. My moment of insight, however, was found in tears as the Holy Spirit awakened my spirit, healing my mind and body from their depression while giving me new hope.

My perspective broadened dramatically. Suddenly, I was able to perceive truths that had previously escaped me. Viewing everything through the lens of the Beatitudes, I found coherence in all Scripture. In this enlightened state, I was liberated from the constraints of my ego. The Beatitudes, embodying the essence of Jesus's teachings, gave me a clear vision of the prophetic rhythms of Elohim's (God, Creator) redemptive narrative. Who I was and my purpose became clear. The Beatitudes awakened an entire universe within.

"No eye has seen, no ear has heard, and no mind has imagined what God has prepared for those who love him."
1 Corinthians 2:9 (NLT)

I found myself no longer just studying concepts but living them. The Celtic Christian idea of "thin spaces" (sacred places where the veil between the spiritual and the material world is thin) became a tangible reality for me. Nature transformed into a sanctuary, and I enjoyed each encounter. Søren Kierkegaard's notion of the "leap of faith" provided a comforting embrace to my intellectual side, offering solace in the understanding that some answers transcend the realm of books and human knowledge. I discovered a knowing in the unknowing.

My new journey resonated deeply with the Desert Fathers, early Christian hermits who left the confines of the structured church to live in solitude, becoming vessels for the Spirit's movement. Their path mirrored my longing to break free from established norms and go deeper into the spiritual essence of my faith, my complete reality, not an essence I only dreamed of. I discovered that silent retreats, even if for the day, awakened me. Daily, I discovered the value of meditation.

I had the privilege of meeting and forming a friendship with Larry Green, a former executive at Coca-Cola who went on to found Cloud Walk. Despite being a relatively recent convert to Christianity, Larry's fervent pursuit of a deeper connection with Adonai (Lord, Master) was truly infectious. Under his guidance and through his ministry, I learned listening prayer (centering prayer), and meditation. By practicing these spiritual disciplines, I found a sense of inner peace that opened my eyes to the expansive horizon of the Beatitudes.

At the core of everything—the essence of life, the pursuit of truth, the prophetic patterns woven throughout Scripture—lies a singular, profound calling: "Everything Jesus." Jesus gives us a compass we call the Beatitudes so we can constantly check our path and orientation. These paradoxes bring us face-to-face with ourselves, our relationships, our purpose, and our God. Just as the lyrics of the hymn "I

Surrender All" suggest, when we truly surrender, Yahweh unlocks the meaning of each Beatitude, unveiling new dimensions of faith and awareness.

Now all glory to God, who is able, through his mighty power at work within us, to accomplish infinitely more than we might ask or think.
Ephesians 3:20 (NLT)

The Chosen

In the movie series *The Chosen*, there's a powerful scene when Matthew assists Jesus, who is preparing to deliver the Sermon on the Mount. When Jesus provides the core of the sermon one-on-one to Matthew, Matthew expresses uncertainty about whether it will be well-received. In response, Jesus describes His sermon as a "manifesto" and clarifies that His purpose is not to evoke sentimental feelings. Instead, He has come to initiate a revolution, not a revolt. He aims to challenge people with a radical shift in their perspective. He emphasizes that He's not here to offer praise for continuing age-old traditions that have been followed for centuries.

A little time passes as Jesus formulates the Beatitudes after the core of the sermon is written. Likewise, He invites Matthew to hear the Beatitudes. In their dialogue, Jesus implies the Beatitudes are a map, saying, "If anyone seeks to find Me, they should seek out those groups."[1] What does Jesus mean?

Jesus had been contemplating the sacrifices made by His disciples to follow Him, including Matthew, who was facing disdain due to his role as a tax collector. He remembered John the Baptist, who was in prison. He remembered Peter, who gave up his fishing business and the comforts of home to follow Him. He marveled at the transformation of each disciple, their sacrifices, and the courage they demonstrated by following Him. Jesus was saying, "If you want to find

Me, find people like My disciples who possess these attitudes." That's where you find Jesus.

******

Insight: Do you want to be significant? Think about it. The disciples followed Jesus. That's all they ever did, yet we talk about them thousands of years later.

Beatitude Code: Faith is the courage to follow Jesus. The Beatitudes are the compass.

Lectio Divina: *"Now faith is the assurance of things hoped for, the conviction of things not seen. For by it the people of old received their commendation. By faith we understand that the universe was created by the word of God, so that what is seen was not made out of things that are visible."* Hebrews 11:1-3 ESV

Introduction

You will seek me and find me when you seek me with all your heart.
Jeremiah 29:13 (NIV)

The Soulful Journey

The Beatitudes teach us to accept ourselves wherever we are right now because that is precisely where we are. They bring us into the reality of who we are, our struggles, our desires, and our beliefs. Jesus taught us the Beatitudes to serve as a guiding compass so we can discover the enlightenment of our salvation.

How to "Max Out" this Book

After each chapter, I recommend you use the scripture selected to practice the ancient art of Lectio Divina. Embrace this time-honored practice to harmonize with the scripture, allowing its essence to flow through you, inviting moments of transcendence and inner serenity.

To Practice Lectio Divina:

- Read the Lectio Divina scripture slowly, silently, and then out loud.
- Reflect on its meaning and how it might relate to the chapter.
- Respond in prayer.
- Rest in silence.
- Repeat or continue as needed.

Meditation

One of the goals of this book is to encourage you to master the art of frequent meditation. Some people refer to their form of meditation as "centering prayer" or "listening prayer." All forms of mediation have a similar form. Here is a good starting place to begin:

1. **Choose a sacred word or phrase:** Select one representing your intention to open yourself to God's presence. I often use "grace," "peace," or "Jesus."
2. **Find a quiet place:** Choose a quiet and comfortable place where you can sit undisturbed for twenty or thirty minutes. Sit comfortably in a chair or on a cushion with your back straight and your feet flat on the floor or sit on the floor with your legs crossed.
3. **Set a timer:** Set a timer for twenty or thirty minutes to signal the end of your practice (I set my iPhone's timer for twenty minutes, although sometimes I go longer).
4. **Begin the practice:** Close your eyes and take a few deep breaths to relax your body and quiet your mind. Focus on your breathing, taking slow, deep breaths. Then, silently introduce your sacred word or phrase and allow it to bring you into a state of contemplative silence.
5. **Let go of thoughts:** As thoughts surface, kindly release them and redirect your focus to your sacred word or phrase. Avoid getting entangled in analyzing your thoughts. Visualize your thoughts as transient clouds drifting by. Refrain from resisting your thoughts. Instead, embrace them, and you will learn to let them drift away through consistent practice. Meditation holds excellent efficacy for the body, mind, and spirit because it permits our whole being, our essence, to find solace within the embrace of the Christ Spirit.

6. **End the practice:** When the timer goes off, slowly open your eyes and sit for a few moments in quiet reflection. Take a few deep breaths, stretch, and allow yourself to re-enter the world around you.

7. **Reflect:** Afterward, take a few moments to reflect on your experience. Consider journaling about any insights or feelings that may linger.

Meditation is about embracing the present moment without chasing expectations. Sit in stillness, focus on a sacred word, and let yourself fully engage in the experience. With practice, you learn to be present, surrender, and trust the process. You will learn through practice to release attachments to thoughts, feelings, and sensations, free from judgment or analysis. Your mind will sometimes wander, so be gentle and patient with yourself. See your thoughts and feelings like clouds that are passing by. Each thought, passing clouds, is an opportunity to return to the presence of Christ's Spirit.

Names of God

In the pages of this book, I will frequently employ the term "Divine" to refer to the nature of things related to God. When I direct my attention explicitly to God, I will occasionally use the following names that have come to identify the many ways we know God:

- **Elohim** (God, Creator)
- **El Shaddai** (God Almighty)
- **Adonai** (Lord, Master)
- **Yahweh** (I Am)
- **The Christ Spirit** (the Holy Spirit)
- **Jesus** (the Incarnation)

Within scripture, "I Am" is a significant name God gave to Moses in the Book of Exodus, specifically Exodus 3:14 when God identifies Himself as "I Am Who I Am." This name suggests self-sufficiency, self-existence, and eternal presence. It signifies a God who is utterly unique, transcendent, and independent of all creation; therefore, the name Yahweh embodies the idea that God is the ultimate being whose existence is not contingent upon anything else. I identify with Yahweh because it evokes within me a sense of relationship. I believe God wants us to discover His presence and name(s) for ourselves.

Awe and Wonder

In *Beatitude Code*, we discover that meditation, scripture, creation, Jesus, and our hearts converge to unveil the boundless realities of Yahweh. Together, they transcend our limited viewpoints and gradually reveal the awe-inspiring presence of the Father, Son, and Holy Spirit. The Beatitudes are a lifelong journey about nurturing a soulful relationship that leads us into the enlightenment of our salvation.

****

Beatitude Code: Accept yourself wherever you are because that is where you are.

Lectio Divina: *"Be still and know that I am God."* Psalm 46:10 (NIV)

Chapter One

THE BEATITUDES

"God can't give us peace and happiness apart from Himself
because there is no such thing."
C.S. Lewis

When Time Stops

The atmosphere around the mountain was thick with anticipation. Each gust of wind carried a cool, tingling sensation as though the air was charged with the promise of the extraordinary. The scent of olive and fig trees mingled with the earthy aroma of sage and wild herbs, evoking an almost mystical ambiance.

There are days when the fabric that separates the earth from the heavens wears remarkably thin, almost transparent in its delicacy. On such days, Yahweh's boundless grace and sovereignty unfurl across the human expanse, a celestial revelation pointing humanity to the enlightenment of their salvation. Today, marked by the cosmos, was such a day.

Jesus, with a demeanor of quiet determination, made His way up the terrain, His footsteps deliberate against the backdrop of wildflowers. As He reached a relatively flat rock, He settled onto the rocky surface, signaling His disciples to gather close.

From the neighboring paths, the crowd began to swell. Men, women, and children hurried, looking for a spot, a tiny piece of earth from where they could see Him and hear Him. There was a shared sense of expectation even though they were unsure what to expect.

Rumors about Jesus had spread like wildflowers after a spring rain. Stories of miraculous healings, of people's lives forever altered, had reached even the most distant villages. Many had only heard stories passed down from neighbor to neighbor, but today, they were here, driven by a potent mix of curiosity and hope.

All eyes were on Jesus. Every heart held a silent question, an unspoken prayer. What would He say? What would He do?

And now, He was here—and so were they.

Jesus sat in serene stillness while the crowds gathered, His head bowed in meditation. As Jesus gradually lifted His gaze to meet the sea of faces, a gentle smile graced His lips.

Every word spoken that day opened doors that traditions and ancient beliefs had long since locked up. His message was destined to echo through the ages, transforming their perspectives and ushering in a renewed consciousness. Jesus would explain how to receive the things of God with radical freedom, things they could never seize for themselves.

Jesus finally broke the silence, speaking with a slow, deliberate tempo as He lifted His arms to heaven as the authority on earth.

"*Blessed are the poor in spirit, for theirs is the kingdom of heaven.*

Blessed are those who mourn, for they shall be comforted.

Blessed are the meek, for they will inherit the earth.

Blessed are those who thirst and hunger for righteousness, for they shall be satisfied.

Blessed are the merciful, for they shall receive mercy.

Blessed are the pure in heart, for they shall see God.

Blessed are the peacemakers, for they shall be called the children of God.

Blessed are those persecuted for righteousness, for theirs is the kingdom of heaven." (Matt. 5:3-10)

Jesus paused, allowing everyone to soak in what He had just said. He lowered His arms slowly as He bowed His head again. As if drawn by an unseen force, every individual in the crowd, whether skeptical or devout, instinctively followed His lead, surrendering to the moment. It was as if the entire mountainside had become a vast sanctuary.

In those moments, a thin space opened, making heaven and earth indistinguishable. It wasn't just words being exchanged. It was a transcendental communion, a sacred dance between the Son of God and mortal souls. The world stood still, and history pivoted on the fulcrum of His message.

As the crowd listened on the hillside, a hush fell over them, a collective stillness that seemed to blanket the air. They had come from all walks of life, each carrying the weight of their own stories, struggles, and hopes. Yet, as Jesus began to speak, something remarkable happened. Thoughts that once raced and tumbled through their minds began to settle, giving way to an inexplicable peace.

The words Jesus spoke were unlike anything they had heard before. Each Beatitude unfolded a new perspective, a way of seeing and being that was foreign yet profoundly resonant. The concepts were radical and challenging and might have sparked a whirlwind of questions and doubts under any other circumstances. But not today. Today, there was only peace—a transcendent, all-encompassing peace that seemed to emanate from Jesus Himself and infuse the very air they breathed.

This was not the peace one finds without noise or conflict. It was deeper, more profound—the peace that can only come from the Spirit of the Living God. It was as if each word Jesus spoke was a balm to their weary souls, a gentle whisper that said, "All is well."

In those precious moments, something shifted within the hearts of everyone present. There was a sense of unity, a feeling of being in harmony not just with themselves but with each other and with Yahweh. It was a glimpse of the "burning bush," a taste of what it meant to be in the presence of Yahweh.

As Jesus's voice carried over the hills, echoing with the timeless truths of the Beatitudes, a shared hope blossomed among the crowd. They wished for this moment to stretch into eternity, for this feeling of peace to never end. In their hearts, they knew this was a turning point, a pivotal moment in their lives. They were witnessing not just a teaching but an unveiling of the kingdom of Heaven right there on the hillside.

All they could do was receive it.

Prophetic Rhythms

Today, we know this section of Scripture where the Beatitudes are found as the Sermon on the Mount. It is called the most profound sermon ever preached. It starts with the Beatitudes. The Beatitudes have a unique rhythm and sound that remind us of the Psalms. As Jesus speaks truth to truth, the words and phrases are melodic and poetic. They feel good to the ear to hear. His words, like a soft persistent breeze, carry wisdom that dances around the edges of our consciousness, beckoning us toward a place of serenity and profound insight.

Getting too wrapped up in our ideas, beliefs, and egos can block the path to deeper understanding and enlightenment. The first Beatitude brings this into sharp focus, urging us to be "poor in spirit." This isn't about lack, but about freeing ourselves from the shackles of preconceived notions and ego. By doing so, we fling open the doors to learning and absorbing truths that were previously out of reach. This is a call to humility and openness, a clear invitation to embrace a journey of growth and spiritual discovery.

The revolutionary wisdom of Jesus reveals how these paradoxes hold the power to radically transform our thoughts, life, relationships, faith, and purpose—a spiritual awakening many of us fail to recognize. Then, in moments least anticipated, Jesus shows up, guiding us to a profound realization of these life-altering truths. Everything happens for a purpose, even reading this book. Raised in the church, I never envisioned myself embracing being "poor in spirit," but now, that's precisely where I find myself.

****

Beatitude Code: We do not seize the things of God. We receive them.

Lectio Divina: "*Brothers and sisters, whatever is true, whatever is noble, whatever is right, whatever is pure, whatever is lovely, whatever is admirable...think about such things.*" Philippian 4:8 (NIV)

Chapter Two

THE ART OF LIVING

"Be that self which one truly is."
Søren Kierkegaard

A Grain of Sand

The Beatitudes are the teachings of Jesus in a grain of sand. These teachings of Jesus hold the keys to understanding the Divine rhythms that pulse through Scripture, history, and the cosmos. They act as a mirror, reflecting our true selves created in *"the image of God"* (Gen. 1:26-27).

Jesus teaches us the Beatitudes as both a journey and a revelation. They are a sacred compass that shows us reality as it truly is and our purpose in it. They bring us face-to-face with our struggles, beliefs, desires, passions, and relationship with God.

The Beatitudes are eight paradoxes taught by Jesus and found in the Gospel of Matthew. They are the preamble to the sermon on the mount when we learn about the heart and mind of Jesus. These teachings are revolutionary, offering a blueprint for following Jesus that turns societal norms on their heads. Each Beatitude begins with "blessed are" and presents a value or attitude that Yahweh blesses, such as humility, mercy, and having a pure heart.

The Beatitudes are a manifesto that emphasizes a way of being reminiscent of Shakespeare's famous phrase in *Hamlet*, "To be or not to be." Each Beatitude blesses us, which means we increase in

Yahweh's presence. To be in the presence of the Lord is the continuum of reality, past, present, and future.

Embracing the Beatitudes invites us on a transformational journey that aligns us with the prophetic rhythms of Yahweh (God, I AM) and creation. This journey explores the heart of Divine wisdom, where truth and love coexist in perfect harmony. By living out the Beatitudes, we engage in a process of discovery, learning who we are by deepening our understanding of who Yahweh (God, I AM) is.

This journey is characterized by a profound shift in how we perceive reality. Through the lens of the Beatitudes, we are invited to view our world and our role within it with an attitude of humility, compassion, and a deep longing for spiritual truth. These teachings encourage us to value what society often neglects or devalues. We learn to see ourselves as "poor in spirit," recognizing our spiritual dependency on Yahweh's grace and as a result, its blessings and strength.

In this light, we are also called to be peacemakers, warriors for justice, embodying a presence of reconciliation and understanding in a world often torn apart by conflict, polarization, and division. This shift isn't just about changing our actions but transforming our very being, becoming naturally who **El Shaddai** (God Almighty) created us to be.

As we walk this path, we find that the Beatitudes are not just ideals to aspire to, but living realities that transform us. They become the rhythm of our daily lives, shaping our actions, attitudes, and understanding of existence. In discovering who God is—His character, love, and justice—we find our true selves reflected in His image; thus, the Beatitudes serve as a map for this spiritual journey, guiding us toward a profound union with Yahweh and a deeper understanding of our role in creation.

"Be still, and know that I am God." Psalm 46:10 (NIV)

This verse is a cornerstone of everything Jesus teaches us. It mirrors the lifestyle of Jesus, who spent His days healing the sick, teaching, and aiding the poor, and after exhaustive efforts, He sought solitude. Being "still" in the context of the original Hebrew in which it was written is more than embracing silence. According to my Hebrew studies, the word for "be still" means surrender, trust, and letting go. Adopting the Beatitudes involves self-emptying to create space within us to be filled.

In moments of stillness before Yahweh, we come to terms with our limitations, acknowledging that not everything is within our control, and we learn to find peace in this realization. There are Divine rhythms in motion, guiding the ebb and flow of life. The Beatitudes offer a way to live harmoniously with these rhythms, teaching us to live aware and ultimately enlightened.

With the Beatitudes, one encounters Divine paradoxes, whispers of the universe where apparent opposites flow into unity like rivers merging into the vast ocean. Here, the meek emerge as inheritors of the earth, and those who hunger and thirst to be everything they were created for find their souls satiated in unexpected abundance. In the delicate dance of these Divine contrasts, one realizes that to mourn is to be comforted, and in emptiness, fullness finds its voice.

The Beatitudes teach us that we are navigating lives filled with contradictions. We are pulled between our human tendencies and our higher spiritual aspirations. Yet, rather than be daunted by these juxtapositions, we learn to revel in them. We learn to enjoy the paradoxical journey, embracing the complexities within us while staying ever curious, seeking to unravel the grand mysteries that lie ahead.

The Beatitudes have taught me that living them out is the art of learning to live perfectly imperfect lives—or, for that matter, imperfectly perfect lives. Just like the Beatitudes, it's a paradox. When you throw a rock into a lake, you see the ripples across the water. When we live in Beatitude, we see the ripples of purpose, identity, and transcendent presence.

Join me with curiosity in your spirit as we bravely traverse the stepping stones of the Beatitudes. Remember, every heartbeat, every breath, and every age signify your purpose. *You* have a purpose. The Beatitudes are not just about decoding the cipher to ancient teachings. It is also about opening our authentic selves, allowing us to live with passion, purpose, and destiny. Please join me on the journey of a lifetime.

****

Beatitude Code: The Beatitudes are the journey of a lifetime that encourages the enlightenment of one's salvation.

Lectio Divina: *Therefore, do not worry about tomorrow, for tomorrow will worry about itself. Today has enough trouble of its own.* Matthew 6:34 (NIV)

Chapter Three

TO BE OR NOT TO BE

"Who am I, this or another,
am I one person today, and tomorrow another."
Dietrick Bonhoeffer

Swinging Bridges

When I was seventeen, I went on a retreat with my church's youth group to West Virginia. On Saturday night, I found myself straying from the path of convention, skipping the planned events, and feeling almost summoned to walk on a mountain trail toward the unknown. Then, destiny led me to traverse a trembling contraption—a swinging bridge suspended high above a meandering stream.

At that moment, I sat on the bridge, my feet dangling as if soaring on the wings of liberation. In all the fullness of night, the resplendent moon cast its gentle radiance upon the undulating mountains, bestowing a celestial glow. Rays of ethereal light intertwined with wandering shadows, birthing a magnificent ballet of stillness and motion. It was as if the very elements of nature had orchestrated a symphony of beauty, harmonizing the tranquility and dynamism of existence.

There I was, a solitary silhouette amid the majesty of creation, and I sensed another presence. I felt no need to cast my gaze elsewhere to the surrounding wilderness, for this presence did not evoke my instinct to defend myself. Instead, time stood still, and in that suspended moment, a newfound liberation washed over me, dissolving fears, aspirations, and longings.

And then, a tender whisper resonated within, and I knew all of this was not by accident as I continued to soak in the splendid masterpiece. Two words emerged, "I Am," and I knew without thought, comment, or the need to explain anything.

Whispers of the Mountains

In the embrace of the mountains,
beneath the veiled canopy of night,
I am in awe, bathed in celestial light.
Countless stars adorn the velvet tapestry above,
Their brilliance beckons, a cosmic symphony of love.

As I gaze upward, my spirit takes flight,
Transcending the boundaries of earthly sight.
Endless galaxies stretch beyond my reach,
An infinite expanse of lessons they teach.

Infinity and eternity dance in the starry haze,
Whispering secrets of the ancient cosmic maze.

This cherished moment resides within me, forever etched in my soul. Years have passed, and I find myself drawn back to those mountains. Almost every day, I feel the sway of mountains calling my name. I need to stop, reflect, remember, and meditate. From sunrise to sunset, I choose to breathe the fresh air of mountains. If not there, then in my soul.

My spirit looks out over the horizon of our lives, seeing mountain range after mountain range disappearing into the smoky mist. I feel awakened, knowing with all of the uncertainties of life that I am not alone. We are not alone. These memories are never too far from my consciousness. They remind me to treat you respectfully because you are my brothers and sisters in this celestial dance of heaven and earth.

David said all that I have come to know thousands of years ago, *"I lift up my eyes to the mountains— where does my help come from? My help comes from the Lord, the Maker of heaven and earth"* (Pss. 121:1-2 NIV). Today, I live on top of a mountain and always remember to stop daily and hear the whispers.

The Matrix

One of my favorite movies is *The Matrix*. It starts when the main character, Nemo, is looking for something, but is unsure what he is looking for. He meets Morpheus, a rebel leader, who offers him to choose between a red and blue pill. Morpheus tells Nemo that he has one last chance because there's no turning back. If he takes the blue pill, it's over. He promises he will wake up in his bed as normal and believe whatever he wants to believe. If he takes the red pill, Morpheus promises him the truth and nothing more.

Nemo took the pill that changed his destiny. He woke up from a deep sleep and, for the first time, saw reality for what it was. He becomes an active participant, no longer an observer. He gets off the couch and starts to live. He joins the adventure. You might say he returns to who he was created to be. He finds out who he is. And with that reality, he discovers he has a purpose. His purpose is not easy. The mission this new life offers is messy, but it becomes everything. Nemo is living, fully alive.[2]

Be True to Yourself

Discovering the essence of life lies in a single, timeless truth, which includes learning to remain true to yourself, meaning who God created you to be. Being true to yourself is a lifetime practice that requires commitment and recommitment moment by moment. Being authentic means being true to your personality, values, and spirit, regardless of the pressure to act otherwise.

You are not a stereotype or a sum of others' expectations. You are one of a kind, authentic, singular you. As Shakespeare wisely stated, "To thine own self be true."

If you are authentic, you are honest with yourself and with others. You take responsibility for your mistakes. You understand you can be wrong. You have learned how to apologize. You have learned to be vulnerable and open-hearted. The authentic person remains open-hearted and teachable throughout life, understanding the importance of setting healthy boundaries, even when toxic situations persist.

Being authentic means making the best of life wherever you find yourself. It means you have discovered your purpose, maybe even a higher purpose. Being authentic means you have developed the discipline and discernment to deal with the twist of living. You have learned how to discern the things you cannot control from the things you have some influence over. You are honest enough with yourself to know everyone has control issues, including yourself. These are usually false expectations you put on yourself and other people.

Being authentic means your reality is based on what is real, not a mirage or delusion of reality. Your reality is a proactive realization that God created the universe and said it was good. This original blessing imparts purpose and meaning, shaping our perception of life as active participants in creation's care and as bearers of responsibility toward one another and our relationship with the Creator.

To be authentic, you will discover the truth for yourself. The problem with truth is it can be a slippery slope. Many have passionately followed a flawed leader, theology, or ideas throughout history. We can be authentically misguided, chasing the wrong thoughts down endless rabbit holes. We can be authentically narcissistic, so self-consumed that we lose the ability to see beyond our self-centeredness. It is even possible to be authentically evil. Genesis talks about the Tree of Knowledge of Good and Evil. There is the reality of evil in this world. Authentic people learn to identify evil and fight against it through its injustice and with spiritual warfare.

Genesis also talks about the Tree of Life and how we must discover the absolute truths of good discovered in it to be authentic. The Tree of Life is Jesus, the Christ Spirit. It is everything good, pure, and right. *"Blessed are those who hunger and thirst after righteousness, for they shall inherit the earth"* (Matt. 5:6 NIV). This Beatitude encourages us to follow in the footsteps of Jesus, the embodiment of true righteousness, rather than succumbing to self-righteousness.

Today, we are bombarded with screens twenty-four-seven, alluring us into deceptive illusions of reality. We can use our screens as tools or become attached to their altered realities. Studies show excessive screen time creates dopamine addiction, meaning you develop a physical and mental need to be fixated, burying your brain in a grave of constant stimulation.

We have a choice, just like Nemo had. The information age presents challenges unlike all other eras of human history, but this challenge to be authentic has always existed. The ancient truths are still as true today as ever. Many things constantly change, and change can be good, but we need to be intentionally aware of each change, so we do not lose touch with the authentic part of us.

Be Who You Are

The primary distraction to being authentic is when we find things to replace God, and without God in our lives, we cannot be authentically who we are. This is the essence of what the Beatitudes teach us. The Beatitudes teach us how to be human. God challenges us to see the reality of ourselves. Søren Kierkegaard said it this way in his masterpiece *The Sickness Unto Death*, "Face the facts of being what you are, for that is what changes what you are."[3]

How, then, shall we live? How do we become authentic? It has a lot to do with how we perceive the world and think—even what we think about. Most of us in the West have developed a dualistic way of thinking. In her book *The Wisdom Jesus*, Cynthia Bourgeault called dualistic thinking a way to read reality from a position of the ego self. "What's in it for me? How will I look if I do this?"[4]

A significant reason for our frequent misunderstanding of Jesus's teachings is our difficulty grasping His non-dualistic approach to life. Jesus's teachings emphasize a non-dualistic approach, an endeavor to lead us away from seeing the world in terms of binary opposites like sacred versus profane or order versus chaos. Instead, He guides us toward a more holistic view of existence where such dichotomies are transcended, encouraging a deeper understanding and unity with the world and each other.

We may fail to grasp many of the more profound mysteries of life in Christ because we do not have the hardware to discover the deeper mysteries of absolute truth. Many of us need a reset, a new operating system to see the world through the eyes and heart of Jesus. This is why Jesus gives us the Beatitudes, to awaken our spirits and renew our minds.

WWJD

Many churches must recommit to teaching prayer, meditation, Scripture, and contemplation. Churches should consider opening their doors twenty-four-seven to help people participate and develop their spiritual awareness. Lighting a candle, kneeling to meditate, and being present is a good start. We must actively create spaces that help us go deeper into the thin places of our souls. We must continually practice the art of centering prayer (listening prayer). By being intentional and practicing the spiritual disciplines, we can experience the mind and heart of Jesus. We must get out of our comfort zone and heal the sick, baptize the lost, feed the poor, minister to the broken-hearted, and help restore those suffering from dysphoric conditions among us. We need a "What would Jesus do" revolution (WWJD).

Ultimate Realization

Embracing and manifesting authenticity finds its ultimate realization in following the teachings of Jesus as outlined in the Beatitudes. Here's how being true to yourself unfolds in the light of the Beatitudes:

- ***"Blessed are the poor in spirit, for theirs is the kingdom of heaven."*** Being "poor in spirit" means the dominant aspect of who you are, your spirit, consciously acknowledging your nature is incomplete without Christ, and is complete in Christ.
- ***"Blessed are those who mourn, for they will be comforted."*** To mourn is to accept your reality and bring Christ into the center of the most challenging aspects of being human.
- ***"Blessed are the meek, for they will inherit the earth."*** To be meek is counterintuitive except to the authentic person who sees the strength in seeking God's will in all things.
- ***"Blessed are those who hunger and thirst for righteousness, for they will be filled."*** Created in the image of God, our heart's deepest desire is to be synchronized with the very heartbeat of God. We inherently want the right things. Our highest nature is striving for justice for ourselves and others as representatives of God's purpose.
- ***"Blessed are the merciful, for they will be shown mercy."*** Being true to ourselves means reflecting God's mercy and forgiveness in our interactions with others. To forgive is the ultimate act of being authentic, following the example of Jesus.
- ***"Blessed are the pure in heart, for they will see God."*** Being authentic means we have good hearts that have been transformed into pure hearts, and God blesses us by allowing us to see the sacred interconnectedness of reality, including the face of God.
- ***"Blessed are the peacemakers, for they will be called children of God."*** Authentic people have the intentional courage

to make a difference, bringing peace to confusion and love to division.

- ***"Blessed are those persecuted because of righteousness, for theirs is the kingdom of heaven."*** Being authentic often invites opposition when we stand up for truth and love.

Since that night on the bridge, I have been passionate about who I am, God's nature, and my purpose. This quest has had some consistent themes: pure joy and mountaintops followed by frustrations and valleys. The more questions I've asked, the more questions each question seems to ask. I have more than once gotten to the point where I said, "That's enough," but I kept going for some reason I cannot explain. I have more than once gotten off course and lost my way only to find my way back. Part of my faith journey has been learning to accept myself for the spirit Elohim (God, Creator) gave me.

All great thinkers throughout history talk about this "inner being" within us who cries out to be heard, to know as we are known. Carl Gustave Jung, the Swiss psychiatrist and psychoanalyst who founded analytical psychology, is attributed with saying, "The privilege of a lifetime is to become who you truly are."

****

Insight: Jesus did not come to make you more spiritual, but rather to make you more human as God created you ("Imago Dei," meaning in God's image). The Hebrew phrase "b'tzelem Elohim" describes being created in God's image and can be interpreted as "shadows of God."

Beatitude Code: Embrace yourself as God created you to be.

Lectio Divina: *"For you created my inmost being; you knit me together in my mother's womb. I praise you because I am fearfully and wonderfully made; your works are wonderful I know that full well."* Psalms 139:13-14 (NIV)

Chapter Four

THE AWAKENING

"Being 'poor in spirit' means being detached from things—being
able to possess goods without being possessed by them.
It means putting people ahead of possessions—and seeing material
things only as instruments for serving God and the needs of others."
James Stenson

Blessed are the Poor in Spirit

E mbarking on the mystical journey through the Beatitudes, we discover a profound revelation: Imperfection paradoxically serves
as a gateway to perfection. We find the unrefined material within our
imperfections for crafting lives filled with compassion, humility, and
profound spiritual depth. As we dive into the first Beatitude, we begin
to grasp that acknowledging our inner imperfections and vulnerability
is the foundational stepping stone toward reaching the pinnacle of our
most authentic selves—becoming children of God, peacemakers, and
perhaps even saints.

The Master Cipher

The inaugural Beatitude, "Blessed are the poor in spirit, for theirs
is the kingdom of heaven," is the master key to unlocking the wisdom
embedded within all the Beatitudes. Through this gateway, profound
revelations emerge, shedding light on the fundamental essence of our

existence, the Divine nature of God, and the initial spark of awareness that guides us toward the profound realization of our authentic selves.

We are like vessels drifting in a boundless sea, yearning for meaning, purpose, and fulfillment. Without God's guiding presence, we find ourselves adrift in uncharted waters, lacking a rudder or sail. We become lost within the labyrinth of our egos, entangled by false expectations of our cultures, fooled by our successes or failures, trapped by unnatural attachments and addictions, and through the creation of false idols, we can veer far from the inner light within (our spirit) that is constantly seeking its destiny.

Intricately created in the "image of God," our nature echoes with a profound truth. Within us are our truest selves. God created us with a desire to discover who we are. We are body, mind, and spirit. Together, body, mind, and spirit constitute our souls. Our souls harbor our strengths and needs. Our needs run deep, and the inaugural Beatitude offers illumination about our true selves, setting the journey of self-realization into motion. The profound sense of wholeness that follows is initiated by our recognition that God is already in every aspect of our lives.

When we embrace the stages of being poor in spirit, we nurture a deep awareness of Adonai (Lord, Master) that saturates every aspect of our daily life. We begin to unearth and live the Divine blessings of the kingdom of heaven in the present moment. This revelation instills within us the unwavering faith to manifest the boundless hope and love that transcends the confines of time and space. Our inner light, our spirit, awakens and assumes dominion over our will, emotions, thoughts, and the entirety of our being, harmonizing seamlessly with the interconnectedness of creation, including its conflicts, chaos, and imperfections.

Reality

Ultimately, each Beatitude has numerous threads that interweave to bind them into a coherent tapestry. Among these threads, one of utmost significance is recognizing that we realize reality itself is unencumbered by illusion or abstraction. To be "poor in spirit" is to profoundly acknowledge our creation by Elohim and the revelation that our truest and most profound self exists wholly dependent upon our acceptance of this reality: God is our Creator.

When we embrace being poor in spirit, this prompts us to strip away the veils of our ego's deceptions. In doing so, we cast aside this egoic mask and confront the contradictions we've long concealed within ourselves, such as the disparity between what we profess to believe and our genuine feelings, including our doubts. To be poor in spirit is to embark on a journey of releasing our reliance on self-fashioned constructs. Instead, we learn to anchor our being in a higher dependence, surrendering ourselves to the ever-present guidance of the Christ Spirit (Holy Spirit) moment by moment.

The term "poor" that Jesus used holds within it a profound significance. It paints a picture of utter dependency, like a needy homeless person relying entirely on another for sustenance and shelter. In this state of spiritual poverty, we recognize our intrinsic need for God's provision, guidance, and grace. Sometimes, this is challenging for those who have never struggled or those who did struggle and see themselves as "self-made."

Within each of us, there exists an innate longing, a profound desire to become all Yahweh has intended us to be. Yet, it is only when we embrace the state of being "poor in spirit" that we begin to unearth the reality of the purpose we were created for. In this humility and surrender, we find the key to unlocking our true potential and realizing the fullness of who we are.

I Am

As we embark on this journey of self-discovery and spiritual awakening, let us remember that our authenticity, completeness, and deepest fulfillment are intricately woven into our relationship with Jesus (Christ's Spirit). In acknowledging our profound need for Jesus, like a dependent person relying on a benevolent provider, we take our first steps toward realizing the boundless reality of our true selves.

In our spiritual poverty, we surrender the illusion of self-sufficiency, acknowledging our dependence on the wellspring of Yahweh. We cast aside the burdens of egoic self-importance, allowing ourselves to be humbled before the gentle yet powerful presence of the Christ Spirit. In this sacred emptiness, we discover the richness of El Shaddai's (God Almighty) kingdom, an abundance that transcends worldly treasures.

The poor in spirit experience Yahweh in the total sense, for they have cleared the clutter of materialistic hearts and self-centered desires, making space for Christ to dwell within. Theirs is a kingdom of heaven in the here and now, permeating every facet of their lives, step by step, over a lifetime. Being poor in spirit permits the Spirit of Christ to flow like a ceaseless river.

Beatitude Code Essentials

- My authentic nature is realized because I am poor in spirit and intimately share my life with "I Am that I Am," Yahweh. *Delight yourself in the LORD, and He will give you the desires of your heart* (Ps. 37:4 ESV).
- Everything in existence bears the Divine imprint of Elohim's creation. I am a steward of what I have been entrusted with. Please grant me the humility to embrace this role with purpose and find profound meaning in it. *As every man hath received the gift, even so minister the same one to another, as good stewards of the manifold grace of God* (1 Pet. 4:10 KJV).
- The wellspring of all knowledge and truth flows from Elohim's creation, Scripture, and the Holy Spirit—the Christ Spirit. I pledge to faithfully uphold the covenants of God's love and truth, refraining from adding to them. *The law of the Lord is*

perfect, refreshing the soul. The statutes of the Lord are trust-worthy, making wise the simple (Ps. 19:7 NIV).

Blessings

Jesus spoke His native language, Aramaic, but also spoke Hebrew. There are two words for blessings in Hebrew.

The first, "Baruch," means "blessed" or "praised." It is commonly used in Jewish prayers and blessings to acknowledge God's greatness, express gratitude, or invoke His blessings upon something or someone.

We learn from studies such as Thorleif Boman's *Hebrew Thought Compared With Greek* that "Baruch" in Hebrew shares a semantic connection with "Beatitude." Both words convey notions of blessings and spiritual well-being. "Baruch" in Hebrew culture and scripture conveys a sense of Divine favor, holistic well-being, and approval. It's not just a simple expression of happiness but a state of being that aligns with God's will and purposes.[5]

To say "Baruch" is to participate in a tradition of acknowledging and venerating the source of all life and goodness. It reflects a worldview in which humans are in constant dialogue with the Divine, expressing thankfulness for God's blessings and seeking to draw nearer to the Divine Presence through acts of worship, meditation, one's values, and the pursuit of justice and peace. "Baruch" is a state of being for those who follow Jesus.

According to the *Brown-Driver-Briggs Hebrew and English Lexicon*, the second Hebrew word "Ashrei" is often translated as "blessed" or "fortunate." It carries a deeper connotation of profound happiness and contentment. It is often used in the Book of Psalms in the Hebrew Bible (Old Testament) to describe the state of being happy, fortunate, or blessed.[6]

In her article "Bless in Hebrew: The Meaning Behind the Word Baruch," author and journalist Estera Wieja wrote, "Blessings, whether given or received, help us recognize God in our lives and draw closer to Him. It is not a recognition of riches, but rather a humble confession that we are not self-sufficient."[7]

"Blessing" means to increase. When we are blessed, the presence of Yahweh increases in our lives. We are conscious of how Yahweh alone increases the goodness in our lives. To be blessed means to live aware and in the presence of Yahweh. To be blessed means to increase in joy and peacefulness. For example, when Jesus said, "Blessed are the poor in spirit for the kingdom of heaven is theirs," He means heaven is increasing in their lives here and now, as well as forever.

****

Insight: The transformative journey of following Jesus elevates our awareness of being "poor in spirit." This is a process and a discovery where we begin to see the sacred in the ordinary and live more "human" as God created us to be.

Beatitude Code: To know yourself is to know God.

Lectio Divina: *"Do you not know? Have you not heard? The Lord is the everlasting God, the Creator of the ends of the earth. He will not grow tired or weary, and his understanding no one can fathom. He gives strength to the weary and increases the power of the weak. Even youths grow tired and weary, and young men stumble and fall; but those who hope in the Lord will renew their strength. They will soar on wings like eagles; they will run and not grow weary, they will walk and not be faint."* Isaiah 40:28-31 (NIV)

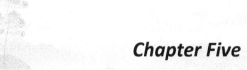

Chapter Five

ROCKY SURFACES

"If you look throughout human history ... the central epiphany of
every religious tradition always occurs in the wilderness."
John F. Kennedy

Do You Need to Yell at God?

I took a four-month sabbatical before September 11, 2001, as a much-needed break from a demanding executive role that had me commuting weekly from Atlanta, Georgia to Los Angeles, California. This period coincided with a significant shift in the computer industry, marked by the rise of the internet and a wave of mergers and acquisitions. During this time, the board tasked me as the senior vice president, along with the president, and interim CEO to manage a massive workforce reduction of 2,800 employees, the sale of our most profitable divisions, and the consolidation of the remaining operations.

Still on sabbatical but beginning to look for another job, sweating on my treadmill while watching CNBC on September 11, 2001, I saw the first plane and then the second crash into the World Trade Center towers. My entire soul melted, and my gaze remained fixed in sheer horror as the once mighty buildings crumbled into dust. It was a moment that stamped us with profound uncertainty. How can it be? It was the same emotion I felt when my fifth-grade class teacher came in crying, saying, "They've killed the president. John F. Kennedy is dead."

I was getting myself re-energized, preparing to re-enter the workforce. The summer before 9/11, I had companies reaching out to me to come to work for them, and I had put them on hold, giving myself some much-needed time off.

Following the tragedy of 9/11, there was a noticeable scarcity of employment opportunities in the computer industry for individuals at my professional level. The global economy and the world itself were undergoing a period of careful assessment and uncertainty.

My history of building effective teams and enhancing profitability garnered me a favorable reputation. However, in the post-9/11 land-scape, I encountered an unexpected challenge. I tried to get execu-tives who had called me in the summer to come to work for them to return my phone calls. They did not. It was a perplexing and disori-enting experience as I perceived my value diminishing. For the first time in my career, I needed a clear path to transform the prevailing confusion into opportunity.

My wife sought guidance from Dick Vigneulle, who eventually became my spiritual mentor. Following our initial session, which lasted no more than an hour, Dick astutely pointed out that I was angry with God. That thought never occurred to me. Still, I listened, although I was certain Dick was wrong. Dick urged me to venture into a secluded space, far from the influence of others, and yell at God, expressing my pent-up emotions and grievances. He emphasized that God uniquely responds to our deepest truths when we are truly honest with our-selves while acknowledging them in God's presence.

Faith Needs Courage

After waiting for several weeks, burdened by the task of con-fronting God, I finally mustered up the courage. I requested my daughter, Shelli, to drive me to a familiar location where I often went backpacking. This specific section of the Appalachian Trail held great significance for me. It was a place my son, Stephen and I had hiked, and a place I had ventured to during my college years, leading a group of twenty-one orphans (ages nine through fifteen) and providing them with a challenging and memorable experience.

After a half-day hike, I reached my destination. I ventured away from the trail to a rocky outcrop that extended over the valley below. As I stood there, I gazed in awe at the breathtaking interplay of colors and shapes in the natural world while confronting the depths of my soul. I felt utterly uncertain about how to begin. I had encountered no one during my hike and no sign of anyone approaching. So, I began to yell. Initially, it was a controlled outpouring of emotions, but gradually, it escalated into a violent release as I unburdened all my pent-up frustrations, heartaches, and fears. I cannot accurately say how long it lasted, but I can say this: If you had been ascending the mountain trail, I believe you would have turned back.

I cautiously retreated from the precipice and found a spot to sit down. At first, there was silence, but strangely, the entire experience felt physically cathartic. Some of my burdens seemed to have lightened. Simultaneously, another part of me found amusement in the situation, almost incredulous at my actions, questioning my sanity and whether Dick's advice was wise. Exhausted, I laughed at myself.

Ruach–The Breath of God

Then, as if propelled by an unmistakable force, a powerful wind of clarity and power spoke to me. Its message was so vivid and compelling that it was impossible to ignore.

This voice was a poignant reminder of how I had often taken control of my life, veering away from God's guidance while paradoxically professing my devotion. God's message to me was crystal clear.

First, I had confused the American dream of building a better life with the life God wanted for me.

Second, in my worldly success, I had, without thinking, begun to see my achievements and possessions as my own. God reminded me everything is His and for His glory—that my gifts and possessions, including myself, were instruments He had blessed me with exclusively for the kingdom of God.

Starting then, I had to embrace a repentant heart, signifying a transformation in my attitude, a quest to find God in every aspect of life, and a total reliance on Him. I did not know what to call this experience, but on that mountaintop, I recognized my most profound need as a human being. I was reminded and became "poor in spirit."

One of the themes of the book is that the journey to know God is a journey of a lifetime. I already knew God before this experience, but I now knew God more intimately. "Poor in spirit" is something we renew every day, our entire lives. You might say it's impossible to follow Jesus until you are "poor in spirit."

Discernment

When God speaks to you, regardless of how it happens, it necessitates discernment and faith. A notable example of this is found in the life of St. Francis. He had a profound epiphany during which the voice of God implored him, "Save My church." Initially, Francis interpreted this as a directive to physically restore the church he was praying in, prompting him to go to his father's store, where he worked, and sell enough fabric to fund the church's repairs, essentially taking from his father without permission. However, he later realized God called him to save the church from corruption and misplaced priorities.[8]

This realization was a transformative journey that spanned twenty-five years, leading St. Francis to become one of the most influential figures in Christianity. He did, indeed, transform the church but never criticized it openly and never became a priest. His reforms came from his teachings and the example he set ministering to the poor. Indeed, when we become the church in the byways of life, the church is reformed.

Voice of God

We hear the voice of God in many ways, with Scripture being one way. The Word of God (scripture) is called "Logos." When God speaks directly to you, this is called "Rhema." It's akin to a gentle whisper from the Holy Spirit, reminiscent of the quiet voice that once spoke to Elijah in a cave. As we grow in our faith through the process and discoveries of the Beatitudes, we begin to sense the essence of God's voice in many ways. When you experience Rhema, sometimes called an epiphany or revelation, you will know.

******

Insight: The Beatitudes cannot be grasped through our minds alone. To be understood, they must be encountered with our spirits and experienced in our daily lives. I encourage you to take a "leap of faith" and practice Lectio Divina and meditation as often as possible. Do you need to go into a closet, a field, or a mountaintop and yell at God?

Beatitude Code: Passionately speaking to God creates the silence in which God's voice is heard.

Lectio Divina: *The Lord is near to all who call on him, to all who call on him in truth.* Psalm 145:18 (NIV)

Chapter Six

WHEN THE MUSIC FADES

"When peace like a river, attendeth my way, when sorrows like sea
billows roll; Whatever my lot, Thou hast taught me to know.
It is well, it is well, with my soul."
Horatio Spafford

Blessed are Those Who Mourn

As Jesus stood before the crowd on the mountainside, His piercing
gaze swept across their faces, taking in the lines of worry, pain, and
sorrow etched in their souls. It was as though He was looking directly
into each person's hurts and pains. He knew that each one there had
experienced suffering, injustice, and death in their daily lives, whether
at the hands of the occupying Romans or through the harsh realities of
long days of hard work, illness, and struggles. He saw their hidden tears.

"Blessed are those who mourn," He proclaimed, "for they shall
be comforted." Like "poor in spirit," no one was expecting that. Jesus
spoke words that seemed to defy logic. Yet, the power of His presence created a beautiful ripple of revelations that washed over them,
uplifting their souls with a sense of profound goodness and joy.

The disciples and the crowd listened intently. Their hearts pounded
in their chests. They knew all too well the pain of losing loved ones,
the struggle to make ends meet, and the constant threat of violence
and oppression. And many secretly mourned their sins, the things
they just didn't seem to have the ability to be free of. Yet, despite
these trials, they tried to cling to hope, a faith they did not always

understand, but somehow, they believed God had not abandoned them. It was as though they had lived to be here, at this place, now.

Here and Now

The anointed words of Jesus speak to our souls. Jesus brings the presence of Yahweh into the middle of our suffering. He promises comfort and healing, redemption and restoration. Because of Jesus, we feel the love of Yahweh. It's a bridge far, yet by faith, we travel it, no longer alone, no matter how long.

Life was, indeed, formidable for the disciples and the people on the mountainside. Yet in the words of Jesus, they found a source of strength and encouragement that would help carry them through, even during times that seemed hopeless. And so, they listened with open hearts and minds. They came looking for something. Despite their entrenched positions and opinions, in the presence of Jesus, many who were unteachable became teachable. Jesus promised them a new way of life, one that was filled with love, compassion, and hope. He was promising comfort where there was none.

The Beatitude to mourn gives us a door to mourn our losses, sins, and disappointments the Jesus way. This does not mean it will be easy or without pain, but if Jesus promises comfort, it will come. One way to effectively mourn is to claim Scripture out loud. If you are suffering, say out loud multiple times per day, "Blessed are those who mourn, for they will find comfort." This becomes a prayer, a promise, and will become your reality. Say out loud other scriptures that resonate with you. My wife and I often claim out loud Psalms 37:1-11. When we hit dead ends, claiming scripture out loud is a constructive way to mourn a difficult situation. It's amazing how God's Word works! After all, it is God's Word, always grounded in truth, love, and power.

The process of mourning is an ongoing journey of learning and growth. Each experience of mourning teaches us valuable lessons about approaching our grief more comprehensively and holistically.

The more we invite Adonai into our pain, the more Christ can utilize our suffering for His Divine purposes and our transformation. Throughout my own life, I have gained insight into mourning various losses, including broken relationships, job and business setbacks, financial hardships, the passing of loved ones, and even my struggles with depression. These experiences have contributed to my ongoing journey of awareness and healing, and Adonai has used me numerous times to mentor people going through the same struggles.

****

Insight: I hold a profound belief that one of the fundamental revelations we encounter along the path of the Beatitudes is the realization that we all possess the capacity to be ministers not in the formal sense, but rather in the manner elucidated in Scripture—utilizing the gifts of the Spirit. In my case, these gifts manifest as mentoring, teaching, and prophecy. Do you know your gifts?

******

The Curveball

No matter how good or bad your life is, life will throw some curveballs you cannot hit. It may be with your health, family, job, finances, security, marriage, children, or even war; it's not a matter of whether it will happen, just when. Jesus is our model. He lived the perfect life, but He faced off with self-righteous church people. They plotted against Him, using all the tools of government, bureaucracy, and religion to destroy Him. He got angry at money changers in the temple. He lost friends. He was betrayed. He was beaten. He died a horrific death on a cross next to criminals. He remained faithful to God's will through it all. He rose from the dead three days later.

Humans will face death, injustices, suffering, and sin. These are the reasons we mourn. To mourn is the second beatitude Jesus teaches us. When we suffer, mourning is essential for our bodies, minds, and spirits. When we need to mourn, we experience a deep pain beyond our natural desires. At this point, only mourning will work. The pain seems overwhelming, and we need something beyond our standard stress-handling methods. Jesus is teaching us that mourning is essential to being authentically human.

Adversity

Adversity upsets our expectations of how we think life ought to be. Sometimes, in adversity, we expect things to turn around and return to how they used to be, and that does happen. We have all heard the stories of how someone faced adversity and turned it into something better, but there are also times when adversity permanently alters our reality, and we must learn to live with it.

Weakness Finds Strength

David and his men returned to their town of Ziklag only to find it burned down by the Amalekites and their families were taken captive, including David's two wives, Ahinoam and Abigail (1 Sam. 30). David and his men were deeply distressed and wept bitterly over their loss. In 1 Samuel 30:6 (ESV), it is written, *"And David was greatly distressed, for the people spoke of stoning him, because all the people were bitter in soul, each for his sons and daughters. But David strengthened himself in the Lord his God."*

David then inquired of the Lord for guidance and received assurance. God instructed David to pursue the Amalekites and recover all that had been taken. David and his men followed Yahweh's Words, rescued their families, and recovered all their possessions. This event demonstrates David's faith and trust in God during a difficult time.

"He gives strength to the weary and increases the power of the weak."
Isaiah 40:29 (NIV)

I can do all this through him who gives me strength.
Philippians 4:13 (NIV)

Your Words Matter

In your wilderness experiences, be on watch against a bitter heart. Your words will be your thermometer. Shortly after the Israelites had crossed the Red Sea and were in the wilderness, they came to Marah, where they found water that was bitter and undrinkable (Ex. 15:22-25).

In response to the people's complaints, Moses cried out to the Lord, and the Lord showed him a tree. Moses threw the tree into the water, and miraculously, the water became sweet and drinkable. This event served as a test of the Israelites' faith and a reminder of Yahweh's provision and care for them in the wilderness.

In the wilderness of sorrow, we must cry to Yahweh and watch the water of our mouths. The mouth is capable of curses and blessings.

The tongue has the power of life and death,
and those who love it will eat its fruit.
Proverbs 18:21 (NIV)

The soothing tongue is a tree of life,
but a perverse tongue crushes the spirit.
Proverbs 15:4 (NIV)

Let your conversation be always full of grace, seasoned with salt, so
that you may know how to answer everyone.
Colossians 4:6 (NIV)

Raise Your Head Up

Abraham was feeling troubled and concerned about the future, particularly because he had no children to inherit the land and blessings promised to him by God. God reassured Abraham by taking him outside and telling him to look up at the night sky and count the stars, saying that his descendants would be as numerous as the stars.

On that day, the Lord made a covenant with Abraham and said, *"To your descendants, I give this land, from the Wadi of Egypt to the great river, the Euphrates*–Genesis 15:18 (NIV).

This promise is known as the Abrahamic covenant.

In your mourning, raise your head with open eyes, and remember El Shaddai is there. We need to physically, intellectually, and spiritually look up when everything else tells us to look down. Therefore, venture outdoors, gaze upon the stars and remind yourself that God created everything and remains with you. This act embodies an expression of faith

"God is our refuge and strength, an ever-present help in trouble."
Psalm 46:1 (NIV)

"The Lord is my rock, my fortress and my deliverer;
my God is my rock, in whom I take refuge, my shield and
the horn of my salvation, my stronghold."
Psalm 18:2 (NIV)

The Voice of Truth

To mourn is the voice of truth within us.

It speaks to the reality that all is not well. Our lives are all bound up in this beautiful kaleidoscope of creation, humanity, and God. As good as it is, there is injustice, death, sin, suffering, and loss. We can try to live temporarily in our comfort, denial, and apart, but that only exaggerates what is wrong. Someone once said, "I tried to hide my hurt at the bottom of a bottle. I tried to hide by working hard. I tried facing it sober. It still hurt." To mourn is to realize the truth, to accept that everything is not all right, and we are hurting because of reality.

Pain is the necessary price we pay for being human. Mourning is the remedy God gives us to face the pain. And because we mourn, we start a process that comforts us and helps us move on and use our pain for good. The blessing is comfort, not that the pain will entirely go away. Comfort here means learning to live with the pain. If a parent loses a child, they will need to mourn and move on to take care of the other children, but they will always suffer the loss.

Either we undergo baptism in the death and resurrection of Jesus, embracing suffering and whole living, or our faith becomes a mere component of a belonging system, lacking the transformative power to change ourselves and the world.

From the perspective of Jesus, mourning is an essential aspect of the human experience, and it involves acknowledging and grieving the world's pain, suffering, and brokenness. In the Gospel of Matthew, Jesus teaches, *"Blessed are those who mourn, for they shall be comforted"* (Matt. 5:4). This teaching suggests that there is a spiritual blessing or benefit that comes from mourning, even though it involves experiencing pain, suffering, and sorrow. This type of mourning is possible because we are also "poor in spirit" dependent on God, and our spirit's consciousness recognizes our pain and the need to take it before Adonai.

Mourning Sin

In the Christian tradition, mourning is often associated with repentance, turning away from sinful behavior, and turning toward God. The Greek word "metanoia," used in Scripture for "repent," means to change one's mind. This involves recognizing and mourning one's sinful actions and attitudes, their impact on oneself and others, and how they separate us from God's presence. Through this process of mourning and repentance, individuals can experience a sense of forgiveness and reconciliation with God and others.

The Beatitude brings us into the reality of our need for a savior. As we learn to grieve over our transgressions and move into a state of grace and genuine repentance, we mourn. We mourn our blindsides, ignorance, sins, and missed opportunities. We come to grips with our truth. At the heart of our condition, we understand what Jesus is teaching us about mourning. We experience it. By acknowledging the reality of our brokenness and our deep-seated need for God, we take a vital step forward on the path of faith that leads us to mourn our sins and empathize with suffering, loss, and injustice in our relationships.

Jesus was known for His compassion and empathy toward those suffering, and He modeled mourning as an essential part of the human experience. He wept at the death of His friend, Lazarus, and He mourned over the city of Jerusalem, which He saw as a symbol of human brokenness and the need for spiritual healing.

From the perspective of Jesus, mourning is essential because it involves acknowledging and confronting the reality of human brokenness and the need for spiritual healing and transformation. Through mourning, individuals can become more aware of their limitations and flaws and seek to live in greater harmony with God and others. Mourning also makes us realize we need to leave room for God. Sometimes, our circumstances, or even our emotions, may seem hopeless. If we mourn without bringing God into the center of our pain, the pain is only recycled. If we mourn with Jesus, we will find a source of comfort.

God is Here

In moments of sorrow, we must pause and mourn,
For losses we bear, in the light of dawn.
Look to the heavens, raise heads high and free,
Seek strength in the Lord, find your solace there.

Avoid bitter words, let kindness freely flow,
For in tongues of harm, no love can truly grow.
Trust in God's goodness, His plan, and His grace,
In Beatitude to mourn, we find comfort there.

In the arms of Jesus, our comfort will reside,
When we turn to Him, in Him, we'll confide.
Mourning may be heavy, the burden may seem vast,
But His love, like a balm, will heal us at last.

****

Beatitude Code: Mourning is the voice of truth that invites God to share our pain.

Lectio Divina: *"The Lord is close to the brokenhearted and saves those who are crushed in spirit."* Psalm 34:18 (NIV) *"Rejoice with those who rejoice; mourn with those who mourn."* Romans 12:15 (NIV)

Chapter Seven

THE SERMON

"There are two days in the year that we cannot do anything,
yesterday and tomorrow."
Mahatma Gandhi

Tears of Reality

During the same year, I had my mountaintop experience, my wife, Sherry, and I attended Perimeter Presbyterian, a church where my daughter-in-law, Sarah, grew up in. Pastor Randy Pope was preaching a series of sermons on the Beatitudes. The first one about the poor in spirit was good, but the second one about mourning touched something deep within me that needed unearthing. Tears flowed down my cheeks when he pointed out there are missed opportunities, we must also mourn.

Oh, boy. I had a big regret. When I was in college, God called me to full-time ministry. It was an exhilarating time in my life. I spent thousands of hours studying Scripture, reading books, meditating, leading groups, and looking for insight. As an eclectic person, I have always drawn inspiration, knowledge, and ideas from various sources, styles, and disciplines. During college, I also had to work to make ends meet and pay my way. I had the energy to do it all.

Before my senior year, I got married. Yet, from the moment I said, "I do," I entered a nightmarish hell. In the days leading up to the wedding, life was filled with intoxicating incense, an effervescent connection, and what I perceived to be love. However, as soon as the vows were exchanged, the enchantment vanished into thin air.

After driving away from the church, the once-promising horizon grew dark and ominous. For the following six months, my life spiraled into an abyss of uncertainty and torment, where every moment was shrouded in bewildering unpredictability. I grappled with a profound sense of betrayal; my world was tainted with confusion and an over-whelming loneliness unlike any I had ever known.

After a mere half-year of marriage, I came home, and everything was gone. She absconded with nearly everything, leaving behind only my clothing. She did leave a bottle of sleeping pills in the medicine cabinet. Unbeknownst to me, I was never aware she took them.

Within my family, I did not know anyone who had ever been divorced. Because I had given my oath to her and God, I wanted it to work out. And yet, there was a demon so pervasive and real that I knew the marriage would consume me and eventually kill me. There was something there that defied explanation: sin, mental illness, demons. To this day, I don't know. My existence had plunged into the depths of despair, anxiety, and bewilderment. I was trying to do everything right, but it didn't matter. I did not know what to do until one day, I came home, and she was gone.

Day after day, I dutifully attended school and fulfilled my work responsibilities, but once the sun set, I found myself at the mercy of an empty bottle.

One fateful night, as I attempted to focus on my studies, my mind remained stubbornly resistant. Sleep, too, eluded my grasp. Desperation guided my hand to the memory of the sleeping pills tucked away in the medicine cabinet. With tentative fingers, I ingested one pill, yet going to sleep continued to elude me. In my desperation to go to sleep, I consumed another, then another, until hours later, I had unwittingly consumed the entire bottle.

Two days later, I woke up from a nightmarish stupor, my breath feeble, my body rigid, and my face ashen like the finest talcum powder.

With tremendous effort, I mustered the strength to make and pour myself a cup of coffee, my trembling hands slowly bringing me back to life as I shuffled through my apartment's dimly lit confines.

My Angel

Suddenly, an unexpected knock echoed through my solitude. At that moment, the last thing I desired was an intrusion. Nevertheless, some enigmatic force compelled me to approach the door, and I reluctantly answered. To my astonishment, it was my dear friend Bill Johnson. I had first crossed paths with Bill a year earlier. A Lutheran pastor on sabbatical, he was my parent's age, but we connected immediately.

One of the most memorable times of my life involved Bill. I extended an invitation to Bill, alongside other friends, on the eve of the 1976 presidential election. As we gathered, the atmosphere was suffused with the rich aroma of wine, and our conversations flowed with the fervent hope for the underdog, Jimmy Carter, to prevail. Bill's brilliance shone through in every word he spoke, his intellect keen, his heart a wellspring of boundless compassion, and his spirit a flame of unquenchable curiosity.

Whenever I found myself in Bill's presence, he possessed an uncanny ability to inspire me to aspire to be a better me. He was one of the first people to encourage me to write. At this juncture, I needed the presence of someone I trusted. It was miraculous that, having returned from California and I had not seen him for over six months, he was standing at my front door – at this moment. God does send angels.

As Bill entered, he keenly perceived that all was not well. We engaged in marathon conversations that stretched on for hours. In a moment of decisive action, he got up, went over to the phone, dialed my father, and candidly laid out the troubling situation. Hours later, my parents arrived, standing by my side with unwavering support. For the first time in a long while, although drowning in uncertainty, I found solace in the undeniable truth that my parents loved me unconditionally and that I had a friend who would always be there for me. Bill and I remained best of friends for over forty years until he passed away.

I had hidden from everyone that my marriage was a nightmare. Getting it out in the open was a first step; however, I remained trapped in the grip of my new identity. It would take several more years of grappling with despair before I could begin to emerge from the abyss that held me captive.

Back on the Pew

As Randy Pope preached about mourning, this heavy rock from my past rolled over. Tears streamed down my cheeks as I remembered those troubled times, reflecting on the missed opportunities amid those harrowing days of my hell. I had given up my aspirations of attending the seminary, and in my darkest moments, I abandoned my education, just shy of completing my last semester. The Divine calling to ministry that once burned within me now lay obscured by the haze of my anguish, leaving me incapable of discerning a viable path forward.

In those tumultuous years, I embarked on a series of endeavors, some with virtuous intent, others mired in recklessness. While I never received professional help or used antidepressants, I sought solace in the refuge of marijuana, using it as a means to numb the pain just enough to continue functioning and working. Yet, even in my outward semblance of functionality, I traversed life as a mere shadow of my former self, feeling incomplete and fractured.

As the sermon continued, I remembered my shame, my disappointments, and how I thought something must have been seriously wrong with me to get married in the first place. I had learned to compartmentalize this part of my life, to feel and act as though it never happened. I never acknowledged it or talked about it. I was ashamed and had never thought to forgive myself, much less her.

During this uncertain period, the teachings of the Beatitudes took on profound significance in my life. God's message became clear: I needed to extend forgiveness to myself and harness the power of my own story to serve His Divine purpose. However, it would take another two decades for this reckoning of my past to materialize here and now. This is why I have chosen to include this story in my book, although I would have rather taken the easier road and not said anything.

Sharing this agonizing chapter of my life remains a formidable challenge. It's a narrative I still find uncomfortable to talk about. However, a remarkable shift occurred when I wholeheartedly embraced mourning, as the Beatitude encourages us to do. I was met with profound comfort and a new revelation. God revealed to me the path forward—to persist in my entrepreneurial endeavors, which allowed me to become a mentor, a spiritual teacher, and a friend driven solely by the purest intentions, without the pursuit of recognition or titles, but rather with a heart dedicated solely to serving God's purpose. And I have tried to do so.

Happy Me

It is important to know how good God has been to me after my hellish experience.

In the following years, my father encouraged me to get to know Sherry, a remarkably gifted pianist who became the love of my life. We married and had two beautiful children, Stephen and Shelli. Today, we revel in the joy of seven grandchildren. My career has been as diverse as my eclectic nature. I've been the director of social work for the Masonic Children Homes. Then, I spent over twenty years in the computer industry, rising to vice president of a Fortune 100 company. Today, I do ministry, write, and own a small company. My life isn't without challenges, but I am exactly where I am supposed to be because that is where I am. Our home rests atop a mountain, a dream I've always dreamed of—a thin space where I still listen—and I am writing, which fulfills me in ways work never could. As it turns out, this is my calling.

****

Insight: At the core of the Beatitudes, Jesus is encouraging us to invite God into the reality of our lives, good and bad. By embracing this invitation, we confront an unadulterated reality in which God is present to listen, guide, and console us. When we attempt to navigate life without God, we violate our very nature, trying to fill life with things that never fulfill us.

Beatitude Code: Radical honesty with God preserves the doors of your heart.

Lectio Divina: *"He does not treat us as our sins deserve or repay us according to our iniquities. For as high as the heavens are above the earth, so great is his love for those who fear him; as far as the east is from the west, so far has he removed our transgressions from us."* Psalms 103:10-12 (NIV) (In this verse, the word for fear in Hebrew signifies our astonishment at how great God is, a profound sense of awe and wonder.)

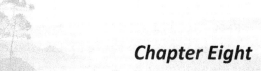

Chapter Eight

THE PAIN BODY

"Therefore, if anyone is in Christ, the new creation has come:
The old had gone, the new is here!"
2 Corinthians 5:17 (NIV)

The Obstacle of Emotional Conversion

We can waste days, weeks, months, and years feeding our pain. In his book *A New Earth*, Eckhart Tolle calls this the "pain body." Tolle defines this as "accumulated pain" and a "negative energy field that occupies your body and mind."[9] The pain body starts a cycle of living with a knee-jerk reaction to the world around you. It seems we are powerless to stop it. We feed the energy and get caught up in it. Doing this only recycles the pain.

The obstacle to effective mourning and forgiveness is often our pain body. As we travel the path of the Beatitudes, we become aware of how each Beatitude forms a synergistic bond with the previous ones. We also learn we must consistently relearn each Beatitude as we live. Just like a recovering addict, relapse is part of the Beatitude's journey. Hopefully, what each of us learns as we travel the path of the Beatitudes is to see the wellspring of blessing in the middle of our most painful situations. It's easier said than done. And it gets easier when we learn to bring God into the center of our pain and release our ego's control over us.

Pain Body

When the pain body is in control, we need to return to the basics. Remember, you are exactly where you are because that is where you are. In Beatitude, during our life's journey, we always deal with reality because our God is the God who created reality.

When we need to mourn, we are always in pain. When we need to forgive, we are always in pain. I used to hear growing up to leave your burdens at the foot of the cross. I never learned how. This was one of the reasons Dick suggested I go into the wilderness and yell at God. I had lost touch with my reality, what resided deep inside, things I had bottled up, fears, sins, failures, secrets, shame, and sins against me. Dick realized I needed to uncork, accept my reality, and have God present. I needed to return to being poor in spirit and mourn and forgive.

Many Christians do not enjoy the freedom of their salvation because of unresolved emotional pain. While they have been converted, their emotions have not. That's why the song "I Surrender All" speaks volumes to our souls. When we fail to surrender all, we seek other means to feel good about ourselves, and we will feel better for a while, but it always spirals back into the pain body.

A New Earth introduced the concept of the "pain body" to describe the accumulation of emotional pain and suffering that individuals carry within them. Eckhart Tolle suggested that this pain body often influences our thoughts, behaviors, and reactions and can be a significant obstacle to experiencing peace and happiness.[10] Here are several insights and practices for dealing with the pain body:

- **Awareness**: The first step in dealing with the pain body is to become aware of its existence. Many people are not conscious of the emotional baggage they carry or how it influences their lives. By recognizing the pain body, individuals can begin to disidentify from it.

- **Presence**: It is important to learn to be present in the moment. Tolle suggested that the pain body is most active when our minds are either dwelling on past traumas or worrying about the future. By staying present and mindful, we can prevent the pain body from taking control. This is one of the values of meditation, to be in the moment.
- **Non-Identification**: Try not to identify with the pain body. Instead of saying, "I am angry," or, "I am sad," try saying, "There is anger in me," or, "There is sadness in me." This subtle shift in language helps create a separation between the individual's true self and the pain body.
- **Observation without Judgment**: Develop the habit of identifying the pain body without judgment or resistance. When negative emotions arise, rather than trying to suppress or deny them, acknowledge them with compassion and curiosity. This non-judgmental observation can help weaken the grip of the pain body.
- **Stillness and Inner Peace**: Practices such as meditation, mindfulness, yoga, and deep breathing can help individuals cultivate inner stillness and peace. Taking long walks and meditation works for me. These practices can reduce the activation of the pain body and create a space for more positive emotions to emerge.
- **Forgiveness and Compassion**: Jesus emphasized forgiveness, both of oneself and others, to dissolve the pain body. Forgiveness allows individuals to let go of the emotional baggage that fuels the pain body and opens the door to healing.

By becoming aware of the pain body, practicing presence and non-identification, and cultivating inner peace and compassion, individuals can work toward reducing its influence and experiencing greater emotional and spiritual well-being.

Enneagram

The Enneagram is a personality system that describes nine different personality types, each with its core motivations, fears, desires, and behavioral patterns. It is often used as a tool for self-discovery and personal growth. Here's a brief description of how the Enneagram can help individuals learn about themselves, especially regarding their "pain body," and how it can be integrated with meditation and the Beatitudes for personal enlightenment:

- **Self-discovery**: The Enneagram helps individuals identify their primary personality type, allowing them to gain insight into their core motivations and behaviors. Understanding one's Enneagram type can provide a more profound awareness of why they react to situations the way they do.
- **The "Pain Body"**: The "pain body" concept, popularized by Eckhart Tolle, refers to accumulated emotional pain and unresolved issues that influence our thoughts and behaviors. By identifying their Enneagram type, individuals can recognize their unique pain triggers and patterns, helping them understand the sources of their emotional pain.
- **Meditation**: Meditation is a powerful practice that can help individuals observe their thoughts, emotions, and reactions objectively. When combined with Enneagram insights, meditation can be tailored to target specific areas of emotional pain and encourage mindfulness and self-compassion.
- **Beatitudes**: The Beatitudes offer guidance on how to live a blessed and spiritually fulfilling reality. Integrating the Enneagram with the Beatitudes can help individuals identify areas where their personality type may lead them away from the path of spiritual enlightenment described in the Beatitudes.

The Enneagram can be a valuable tool for individuals seeking self-awareness and personal growth. Combining Enneagram insights with meditation and the Beatitudes can help individuals better understand their pain triggers, work through unresolved issues, and find new awareness and enlightenment on their Beatitude journeys.

The Enneagram played a significant role in my Beatitude journey, pain body, and transformation. I believed so much in the Enneagram I became an Enneagram coach. On my Substack, stevebruner.substack.com I write how to integrate the Beatitudes and the Enneagram.

****

Encouraging Advice: Sometimes, we may need professional help if our pain body has control over us. It happens. It happened to me. I got help. If you need it, please seek professional help.

Insight: When we experience pain, finding solace lies in the practice of reading God's Word aloud, a process often referred to as "claiming God's Word." While my wife and I have seen miracles from this practice, the most important thing that happened was our attitudes learned to face our pain with the peace of Christ in our hearts, and everything seemed better even though in some instances, it was not. Sometimes, the most uncomplicated and simple acts of faith provide the blessing.

Beatitude Code: Claim Scripture out loud, infusing God's Word into the promises of your heart.

Lectio Divina: *"Come to me, all who labor and are heavy laden, and I will give you rest. Take my yoke upon you, and learn from me, for I am gentle and lowly in heart, and you will find rest for your souls. For my yoke is easy, and my burden is light."* Matthew 11:28-30 (ESV)

Chapter Nine

THE GOD THING

*"Do not conform to the pattern of this world but be transformed by the renewing of your mind. Then you will be able to test and approve what God's will is—his good, pleasing, and perfect will. "*Romans 12:2 (NIV)

Blessed are the Meek

A s Jesus turned His gaze away from the multitude, He looked deeply into the eyes of each of His disciples. He said gently and authoritatively, "Blessed are the meek, for they shall inherit the earth."

The people speculated if Jesus was laying the groundwork for a revolution. In unanimous consensus, they yearned to overthrow Roman rule, perceiving it as a common need. To their collective dismay, many of their religious leaders had appeared to compromise their integrity by aligning with the existing authorities. It was a sentiment rooted in a deep longing to return to the era of strong leaders like David, a time they fondly remembered as the "good old days."

The presence of Jesus, though, was nothing short of overwhelming. His words carried an unparalleled authority, yet He did not project the image of a military or political leader, leaving them somewhat perplexed. They had already begun to discern that Jesus operated on a different plain of logic. It was becoming increasingly apparent that their conventional way of thinking did not always align neatly with the profound perspective that Jesus brought. "Jesus logic" is uniquely His own. When one begins to truly hear the teachings of

Jesus, one realizes Jesus is imparting lessons entirely nuisance to traditional wisdom.

As they listened to Jesus, an understanding began to dawn upon them. The sermon they were hearing was more than just a compilation of catchy phrases. Whatever He spoke of was nothing short of revolutionary, yet it wasn't the kind of revolution they had previously envisioned. It was akin to a roadmap, a guide for embracing a life of genuine blessedness, whatever that means. Now, a pivotal choice lay before them. Would they choose to follow Jesus on this transformative journey, or would they discover that His teachings didn't align with their expectations and needs?

Just As I Am

However, a striking realization dawns upon everyone in attendance: Jesus possesses an extraordinary understanding of all of us. He sees everyone for who they indeed are and approaches them with an unwavering commitment to their well-being. He extends His embrace to us, complete with our imperfections and limitations, even when we may not fully grasp who He is.

We often approach Jesus with preconceived notions and rigid expectations, but still, He exhibits remarkable patience, waiting for the moment when our understanding begins to illuminate, patiently waiting for the light within us to turn on.

In His boundless love and profound wisdom, Jesus possesses an innate understanding of what we require and when we need it. He stands ever-prepared to unveil the enigmatic depths of God's mysteries, elevate our consciousness, and unveil the genuine essence of reality.

As we nurture and deepen our relationship with Him, Jesus naturally becomes our primary focus—an entryway into the very heart of creation and a gateway that leads us to the full realization of the boundless potential of our salvation.

Truly, the magnificence of Jesus emanates from His resolute dedication to shepherding us along the path of enlightenment. He is the radiant beacon that dispels darkness from our journey, the unwavering wellspring of hope that nurtures us, and the origin of all authentic beauty and goodness.

Though Jesus had only just begun to speak, a deep and profound sense of the sacred began to envelop everyone in attendance. It was as though God's Divine presence graced the hillside, transforming this simple location into a sanctuary of unparalleled significance. Here, there were no grand temples or awe-inspiring cathedrals. Instead, it was an ordinary hillside where time seemed to suspend its march.

With each utterance that fell from Jesus's lips, something deep within each listener stirred, and an overwhelming sense of awe washed over them. Once shrouded in the cloak of shattered dreams, their spirits were now revitalized and fully awakened into the present moment. For some, this surge of life coursing through them was an experience entirely novel and profoundly transformative.

As the people leaned in, a sensation washed over them as though the ethereal curtain separating heaven and earth had dissolved, granting them a fleeting glimpse into the Divine realm at that very moment. It was an instance of utter and flawless harmony, where the inherent goodness of the universe unfurled and became manifest before their eyes.

In that sacred instant, their hearts were filled with wonder, yearning for the perpetuation of this timeless moment. Within this hallowed space, they felt an unbreakable connection to a greater, all-encompassing force of love and radiance that suffused everything in their midst.

Are You Meek

There are many interpretations when it comes to the concept of meekness. Some view it as a sign of weakness while others who Jesus has touched see it as an expression of fortitude and strength.

The question now falls to you. What do you perceive as being meek? Would you say you are meek? Do you want to be meek?

Jesus, as always, leads us to the edge of our cognitive limitations, testing our thought processes and the integrity of our beliefs. Once we open our hearts to Jesus, we transcend the limitations of everything we think we know. New horizons, dimensions we never knew, open to us. Being meek is one such dimension.

With Jesus as our guide, we embark on the ultimate pilgrimage of life, leaving behind the life of a mere tourist passing by and embracing the life of faith as a pilgrim in the new covenant.

On this sacred journey, we find ourselves truly alive, embracing each moment with an unwavering passion and a renewed sense of purpose.

Teachable

How can we cultivate an understanding of these teachings and weave them into the very essence of our existence? Our deepest desire is not merely to grasp them intellectually but to honestly know and experience them, allowing them to become an integral part of our being.

To be meek, we must be teachable.

When Jesus expounded on the concept of meekness, His audience consisted of people from rural backgrounds who were intimately familiar with the notion of a meek horse. A meek horse was a creature that had been skillfully trained, possessing both strength and the ability to respond to the guidance of its master.

The Roman occupiers who held sway over their lands boasted an array of formidable horses. These Roman officers rode spirited stallions—swift and powerful steeds meticulously trained for combat. The idea of a meek horse held special significance, signifying a trustworthy and dependable companion even in battle.

God creates us with spirited souls, giving us unique gifts and shaping us in His Divine image. However, we find ourselves at a crossroads, faced with an essential question: If we are not inherently meek, how do we cultivate meekness? This introspective journey leads us to the crux of the matter, the query that demands our unvarnished honesty. Do we truly desire to be meek?

In its purest essence, to be meek signifies a person who diligently pursues God's will in every aspect of life. When viewed through this lens, it becomes evident that meekness is far from a sign of weakness. Being meek embodies strength.

Once more, we are reminded of the Divine sequence of the Beatitudes. It becomes apparent that embracing meekness is intrinsically linked to first being poor in spirit and having the ability to acknowledge and mourn one's sins. Being meek naturally flows from our growing awareness of our spirit and the Christ Spirit.

Tourist or Pilgrim

Being meek means you desire to discover and follow God's will, just like a meek horse obeys its master.

Scripture consistently teaches that God's will inherently serves our best interests. Nevertheless, we often grapple with the temptation to confine God within our limited framework, erroneously believing that we can summon Him only when we require something. This behavior, in essence, reflects the distinction between being a mere tourist and becoming a devoted follower of Jesus and His teachings.

In His calling, Jesus beckons us to be pilgrims rather than tourists on our faith journeys, inviting us to fully engage in the transformative process of embracing God's Divine Will as our guiding compass.

Jesus followed the will of God perfectly. Being meek helps us follow in the footsteps of Jesus. We do not have to strive for perfection. All we must do is follow Jesus. Following the teachings of Jesus is God's will. Learning to emulate and practice the attitudes and ideas of

Jesus is God's will. They become contagious and restore our authentic selves as God created us to be.

A Consuming Fire

To follow the Beatitudes is to embark on a journey of deconstruction of the ego and reconstruction of the self in God's image.

The Apostle Paul says in Hebrews 12:29 that *"our God is a consuming fire."* When we have embraced being "poor in spirit" and the radical honesty of mourning, we begin to see the layers of our ego-centeredness being consumed by God's fire. God's fire is the sovereignty of Adonai's (Lord, Master) Grace—love. It transforms our spirits into the refined metals of humility and generosity.

God's love is a transformative flame, requiring continuous fuel to maintain its vitality. If you jump into the middle of a physical fire, it has the power to destroy. Similarly, the Divine flame of God can rapidly burn away illusions of self, exaggerated notions, egoism, and self-absorption. Surrendering to the spiritual blaze of God's love will consume what the ego clings to, leaving behind only the unadulterated truth of your being.

God's love is a school of fire. This is the path of the Beatitudes. When we glaze through this luminous fire, we discern a visage—the face of Christ. We see Christ longing to use our minds, eyes, hands, and all of who we are to complete His work. Ironically, our role in completing His work is a small part, but that small part completes us as we were created to be.

Fire is mentioned over 500 times in Scripture and 90 times relating to the nature of God. Fire is seen as a symbol of purification, transformation, and rebirth. When Jesus started his public ministry, He went to John the Baptist to be baptized. John said, *"I baptize you with water for repentance. But after me comes one who is more powerful than I, whose sandals I am not worthy to carry. He will baptize you with the Holy Spirit and fire."* (Matthew 3:11).

When we begin to experience life from this perspective, we realize to do God's will is to live into God's will. Essentially, the Beatitudes are a compass to following Jesus which is God's will. And, if we do, God's will stops being some grandiose mystery and is naturally revealed– sometimes in extraordinary ways but most of the times through the ordinary. As we follow Jesus' path, what early Christians called "The Way" the fruits of the Spirit manifest within our everyday lives, transforming the ordinary into the extraordinary.

"But seek first his kingdom and his righteousness, and all these things will be given to you as well" (Matthew 6:33). Seeking righteousness is seeking harmony within yourself, your relationships, and God. Jesus teaches us the importance of prioritizing God's kingdom. This prioritization is the key to discerning God's will.

Life, under the governance of God's will, is indeed a sequence of new beginnings. Each day offers a new opportunity for growth, learning, and transformation. Mistakes and past experiences serve as lessons rather than anchors. Our humanity propels us toward a future where we can reflect God's love in the world.

God's love is a flame that is enduring and unextinguishable. This celestial fire purifies, eliminating that which separates us from God, enabling us to forgive as we are forgiven, for God's Spirit is ceaselessly coming to life within each of us.

Christ-Centered or Ego-Centered

Seeking meekness can prove to be a formidable endeavor. Ego-centered Christians may struggle with meekness because their desire is for God to align with their own will rather than vice versa. Even for Christ-centered Christians, practicing meekness still presents its own set of challenges.

Meekness demands a profound level of self-reflection, a journey that necessitates engaging in spiritual disciplines such as meditation, fasting, worship, acts of charity, immersion in Scripture, and dedicated prayer. Eventually, the meek learn what Paul called "prayer without ceasing," which helps to keep us in the center of God's will.

Our self-righteousness often obstructs our path. It's essential to recognize that being in the center of God's will doesn't automatically equate to flawless execution of His will. In all reality, it's quite likely that we fall short in this regard. However, centering our lives within God's will is the process of developing a heart that seeks God's will and, at the same time, accepts our limitations. The profound strength of faith lies in our willingness to leave room for God to work. By doing so, we stop struggling to find God's will and learn to abide patiently within it.

Remember, it is God's will, not our own, and once we invite the Holy Spirit into our spirit, we can relax in God, which is God's will. We do not have to approach God's will with perfectionism or like it is something we must chase. Once the Christ Spirit has taken up residence within our spirit, God's will is infused into our being, who we are. We naturally are open to it, and it finds us. Some of us call this a "God thing."

Humility

From a Jesus-centered perspective, humility can be understood as the state of being meek. It is characterized by a profound sense of selflessness, modesty, and a wholehearted readiness to align one's own will with God's Divine will. Humility entails the humble recognition of one's limitations, weaknesses, and imperfections, all while acknowledging God's sovereignty and supreme authority.

In line with Jesus's teachings, humility is unmistakably defined by a sincere concern for the well-being of others, a willingness to serve selflessly, and an absence of arrogance or pride. It's about cultivating a humble heart and a genuine commitment to prioritize the needs of others over one's own, much like the example set by Jesus Himself through His life and teachings.

The Honest Challenge

In my role as a mentor, I've had the privilege of supporting numerous individuals through the tumultuous landscapes of their emotional lives. There is a common thread among them to grapple with the quest for understanding God's will for their lives. What often became apparent was that many of them found themselves ensnared in the pursuit of their expectations and desires, rather than genuinely seeking to discern God's will. Until they gained a Christ-centered perspective, their view of God's was like a yo-yo. It was only when they let go of these self-imposed expectations that they were able to discover the freedom they needed to know God's will.

The most profound leap of faith lies in recognizing that God's will inherently parallel what is best for us. I struggled with this type of trust most of my life. This journey can sometimes be daunting, but it remains attainable through unwavering faith. There are moments when we wake up and put on our shoes while declaring, *"Today is a day the Lord has made. I will rejoice and be glad in it"* (Ps. 118:24), which is, indeed, God's will. When we embrace life's flow, the clarity of God's will reveals itself. Sometimes, God's will is something big. Most days, it is discovered in the ordinary, and then life becomes extraordinary.

Sovereignty of God

Being meek is the ultimate realization that God is in control no matter what. Always has been and always will be. This realization brings us into the reality of God as Creator, Redeemer, Almighty, and Author of our history.

When we choose to be meek, we acknowledge the sovereignty of God. The sovereignty of God is easy to for us once we understand it is "everything Jesus."

****

Beatitude Code: The meek discover true strength in God's will.

Lectio Divina: "For the word of the cross is folly to those who are perishing, but to us who are being saved it is the power of God. For it is written, *"I will destroy the wisdom of the wise, and the discernment of the discerning I will thwart."* Where is the one who is wise? Where is the scribe? Where is the debater of this age? Has not God made foolish the wisdom of the world? For since, in the wisdom of God, the world did not know God through wisdom, it pleased God through the folly of what we preach to save those who believe.... For consider your calling, brothers: not many of you were wise according to worldly standards, not many were powerful, not many were of noble birth. But God chose what is foolish in the world to shame the wise; God chose what is weak in the world to shame the strong; God chose what is low and despised in the world, even things that are not, to bring to nothing things that are, so that no human being might boast in the presence of God. And because of Him, you are in Christ Jesus, who became to us wisdom from God, righteousness and sanctification and redemption, so that, as it is written, "Let the one who boasts, boast in the Lord." 1 Corinthians 18-21, 26-31 (ESV)

Chapter Ten

BODY, MIND, AND SPIRIT

"God creates out of nothing. Wonderful you say. Yes, to be sure, but he does what is still more wonderful: he makes saints out of sinners."
Søren Kierkegaard

Who Am I

H uman beings are body, mind, and spirit. This is the sum of our total person, who we are. Our life, all of who we are, is our soul. Your soul is the life God breathed into you. Scripture refers to the condition of our soul as "the heart." The heart is referenced over 900 times in Scripture. Scripture constantly reminds us of the importance of being authentic, who God created us to be.

> *"Create in me a pure heart,*
> *O God, and renew a steadfast spirit within me."*
> Psalm 51:10 (NIV)

The heart implies the conscious aspects of our being, will, emotions, bodies, and spirit. We were created to be holistic, complete, and fulfilled. Every choice we make flows out of what is in our hearts. Life's significance is determined by the choices we make and the attitudes we adopt.

"Above all else, guard your heart, for everything you do flows from it."
Proverbs 4:23 (NIV)

In the Hebrew language, "lev" translates to "heart." However, within Hebrew culture, "lev" does not represent the center of emotions but rather the origin of one's thoughts.

This understanding alters our interpretation of numerous scriptures. For example, when Jesus instructs us to "love the Lord your God with all your heart..." (Matthew 22:37), He is not advocating for a purely emotional devotion to God. Instead, He emphasizes the importance of keeping God-centered in our thought life. Our love for God should influence our thinking and shape our perspective of the world.

Body

The human body has awareness through its functions and the five senses. Smell. Taste. Sound. Sight. Touch. We know a lot today about how each of these senses works. The senses have much to do with our survival instincts and everyday functions like eating. They also have much to do with our pleasures, such as hearing beautiful music, seeing a sunset, or smelling a rose.

Scripture sometimes refers to our bodies as the flesh. The body is the instrument God gives us to enjoy life. The Greeks believed the body was the lowest part of our nature. The Hebrews, followed by the Christians, believe the body is something to be honored. As God says in Genesis about creating male and female, "It is good." This is a biological truth.

When you follow Jesus daily, your body is the temple of the Holy Spirit. Your body (your flesh) can be used for good or evil. Most sins of the flesh are sins against yourself, and in one way or another usually involve others. These sins put unnecessary obstacles in your path to being authentically who God created you to be. Likewise, we honor ourselves and God by taking care of ourselves.

Mind

We have a mind, our thought center, and where our will originates. Just as your fingerprints are unique, all minds are unique. The mind is where our consciousness lies. Each of us is conscious of our existence because of the activities of the mind. The mind's consciousness is associated with cognitive processes such as thinking, reasoning, perceiving, and the ability to be aware of the external world.

****

Insight: The spirit's consciousness, on the other hand, is often described as a deeper, more intrinsic sense of being and awareness that transcends the analytical functions of the mind. It is associated with one's inner essence, soul, or that part of us that connects to the higher power, something greater than ourselves—God and the universal consciousness. When the mind's consciousness conflicts with your spirit's consciousness, this can be a major source of internal tension. When this happens, your will becomes confused and is tossed about like a boat in turbulent waters. Your body, mind, and spirit are not in harmony.

****

Your will is the deliberating center of your mind. We are increasingly learning there are many types of intelligence humans are born with. Our minds are a fantastic gift. The mind can be used for good and evil. Thoughts can be pure and deceptive. Satan attacks our minds if the body does not succumb to addictions. Scripture says, *"work hard to show yourself approved"* (2 Tim. 2:15), indicating how authentic people constantly renew their minds. We can get lost in our minds. If we follow Jesus in Beatitude, our minds find fertile soil to flourish.

****

Spirit

Each of us has a spirit. Watchman Nee, a Chinese Christian teacher in his comprehensive work *The Spiritual Man*, said, "The spirit is the noblest part of the human person. It occupies the innermost area of our being."[11] The spirit is the part of us that senses and can know God. *"Do you not know that you are God's temple and that God's Spirit dwells in you?"* (1 Cor. 3:16 ESV). The spirit lies beyond our self-consciousness. Our spirit elevates and unites us. It is our connection to God.

The writer of Proverbs tells us that *"the spirit of man is the lamp of the Lord"* (Prov. 20:27). God created each of us with the intention that our spirit would be the dominant part of our being, but often we let our bodies and minds dominate our spirits. This creates tension within us. This is why self-righteousness is a dangerous sin because it puts the self, the ego (mind and body), in control, not our spirits, in communion with the Christ Spirit. When our spirits yield to the Christ Spirit, we discover radical freedom to be authentic. This is what the Beatitudes are all about.

Just as we all have different mental and physical attributes, I am convinced we are born with unique spiritual abilities that reflect how God made us. And when we invite the Holy Spirit into our lives, those natural gifts inherited from God flourish under the guidance of the Holy Spirit. The circle of life is complete.

"Now, with God's help, I shall become myself."
Søren Kierkegaard

Conscious Spirit

Our spirit has three functions. One of these functions is spiritual consciousness. The mind has its consciousness. When it agrees with your spirit's consciousness, you experience the peace of God. The mind tries to justify our thoughts and actions that do not agree with our spirit. In other words, our thoughts and feelings can fool us. This creates tension within. Our spirit's consciousness helps us determine what is right or wrong. Our spirit's consciousness works when our spirit is in tune with the rhythms of the Holy Spirit. Being authentic means your consciousness keeps you aware, aware of absolute truth. David says, *"Put a new and right spirit within me."* (Psalms 51.10)

Intuition Spirit

Our spirit also has Intuition. Our spirit's intuition senses God's heart and mind and what God is doing in and around us. The revelations of God and the movements of the Holy Spirit are known to believers because of our spirit's intuition. Intuition is diametrically different from the physical senses and what our minds think or feel. Spiritual intuition is like a compass. Sometimes we think and feel we must go this way, and our spirit informs us differently. This is always the higher road, and the spiritual disciplines awaken our spirit's intuition. When our spirit has intuition, some call this a "God thing" because things happen – and we notice them. This aspect of faith always reveals God in small, big, and ways we do not know, but our spiritual intuition senses it even when we do not see it. We sense God's Presence in our circumstances, in and around the events of our lives.

Communion Spirit

The third function of our spirit is communion. Communion is being in a relationship with God in a spirit of worship. God is comprehended in our spirit by communion. Our spirit is elevated and enlightened when we commune with God in worship. We are refreshed, renewed, fulfilled, and made whole when we worship. Our thoughts, intentions, or feelings cannot comprehend God. We can know a lot about God without knowing God. I can describe riding a motorcycle but riding one, feeling the wind, the speed of curves, and exhilaration. That's experiential. Scripture says, "The true worshipers will worship the Father in spirit and truth." (John 4.23) Holy Communion, the Eucharist, is a Divine blessing and brings us into communion with everything Jesus. John Wesley implied we should participate in communion as much as possible. Communion and worship are not limited to established religious practices. I can worship riding down the road listening to anointed music. Communion renews all of us, body, mind, and spirit. In other words, worship completes who we are.

Essence and Reality

I have come to appreciate how my understanding of essence and reality has shaped my mind and my spirit. Essence and reality have been central to philosophical inquiry across various traditions and historical periods. Works that discuss these concepts often explore metaphysics, ontology, and epistemology, exploring the nature of being, existence, and the fundamental characteristics of reality.

Here's what I've learned. René Descartes examined the nature of reality and the essence of the self, famously concluding with "Cogito, ergo sum" ("I think, therefore I am") as an indubitable foundation for knowledge. Immanuel Kant differentiated between phenomena (the world as we experience it) and noumena (the "thing-in-itself"), discussing how our understanding of reality is shaped by the structure of our minds.

Here's my understanding of essence and reality:

Essence

- Essence refers to the fundamental nature or intrinsic qualities that define something. It is the core set of attributes, characteristics, or properties that make an object, concept, or entity what it is. We experience God's essence in nature because God is the Creator of the cosmos. Nature is not God, but it reflects a characteristic of His essence.

- Essence is often considered as the ideal or perfect representation of something, capturing its essential features without any external or accidental qualities.
- It is a concept used in metaphysics and philosophy to understand the underlying nature or identity of things. The essence of a rose is its fragrance.

Reality

- Reality pertains to the actual state of existence, the tangible and empirical world we experience through our senses. It encompasses everything true, regardless of whether it conforms to an ideal or conceptual essence.
- Reality includes the physical world (e.g., objects, events, phenomena) and the abstract world (e.g., thoughts, concepts, ideas), as long as they exist in some form. It is a broader concept, encompassing the concrete and tangible aspects of existence as well as the conceptual and abstract aspects.

God is the Creator of the cosmos, the very foundation of our reality. We move and sense the essence of God because of creation. It's one of the ways we know God. God's creation is also reality. God ultimately is the reality of realities.

The Beatitudes usher us into a profound state of authentic self-awareness, guiding us to recognize our true selves and understand the nature of God. They reveal the Divine essence is present in everything around us – in the wonders of nature, within our souls, and throughout the arts. As we evolve along the journey of the Beatitudes, our perception of the world becomes ever more aligned with its true state, deepening our appreciation for God's essence. This understanding transcends dualism, embracing a non-dual perspective that is not about choosing the reality of God over God's essence, but about embracing both simultaneously.

Zen

Zen has emerged as a cornerstone of the New Age movement, gaining significant prominence. On platforms like Amazon, the number of books on New Age spirituality rivals, if not surpasses, those related to Christianity. But why is this the case?

The answer lies in the inherent human longing for spiritual fulfillment—a desire that God instilled within us when we were created. It's the quest for a spirit that finds its ultimate satisfaction in the presence of the Christ Spirit (often referred to as the Holy Spirit). This universal yearning draws people toward exploring various paths, including Zen, in their pursuit of a deeper connection with the Divine.

This may explain why an increasing number of individuals are turning to Zen. Zen serves as a life philosophy centered around meditation. Through meditation, we acknowledge the reality of our spirit, embarking on a journey that unites the mind, body, and spirit, even if just for a few moments when practiced.

Zen imparts the wisdom that the ego functions as a mask, concealing our true selves, and emphasizes the importance of focusing on what is truly essential. Its logical perspective recognizes that God's essence permeates all of creation, like Divine DNA woven into the fabric of our surroundings. Through meditative pauses, we can tap into the core of this Divine reality, heightening our awareness.

Zen places a significant emphasis on mindfulness, and the act of meditation itself elevates something profound within us. Here lies the irony: I believe that Jesus stands as the most outstanding Zen teacher of all time. He imparted teachings of ultimate awareness and ultimate truth. For those seeking inner fulfillment, Jesus guides us beyond mere essence, leading us into the realm of ultimate reality.

Jesus imparts to us the profound teachings of the Beatitudes, a treasure trove of hidden mysteries and precious gems that enable us to unlock the Divine power residing within our spirits. Through the empowerment of the Holy Spirit, we embark on a journey toward the enlightenment of our salvation.

Salvation, however, transcends our mere essence; it represents the pinnacle of reality and ultimate awareness. It encompasses everything we have been, are, and will become. It is the sum of our past and future, beautifully wrapped within the present moment. Salvation isn't just a journey or a destination. It is both, an inseparable fusion.

Furthermore, salvation isn't something to possess, but rather a gift to be shared with others. It remains perpetually fresh and new, renewing itself each day. In this way, it's not about accumulation, but about a salvation that is continually renewed and received. John Wesley, the founder of Methodism, had a nuanced view of salvation that emphasized an initial moment of justification by faith as well as being saved every day. In his sermon "The Scripture Way of Salvation" (Sermon 43), Wesley expressed a belief that salvation is not a one-time event, but an ongoing experience of God's grace.[12]

Fire

I love backpacking. I find solace hiking up and down the Appalachian Trail as my spirit communes with God with each step I take. Backpacking mountains is physically challenging, yet my spirit is in constant meditation. I am giving everything I am in time alone with Christ and creation. You might say it's Zen. When the daylight starts to fade, I pick a spot to camp, hopefully with breathtaking vistas where I can see the surreal and magical night sky embraced by solitude and uncertainty. Backpacking is an act of faith in who I am in God. I must trust my joy and my survival to a higher power. It's the most complete worship experience I know.

As the night draws closer, part of my ritual is building a fire. The flames imbue a profound significance. The fire radiates an ethereal illumination, instilling a comforting warmth as I relax, enjoying its transcendent essence. It envelops me in a profound sense of belonging, providing solace and an opportunity to revel in the present, just being there in the moment. Its mystic power dissolves my apprehensions, making me feel whole again. It's as though another person is with me.

Zen is the essence of spiritual energy, the meditation that has been with me since early morning and now rests by the fire. I sit around the crackling fire, fully immersed in the present moment. I am at peace with my surroundings, my authentic self, here and now. It was a long day spent hiking the rugged mountain trails, navigating the ups and downs with sheer willpower, finding water, and avoiding danger. Amid the journey, I crossed paths with a bear, avoided a rattlesnake, savored the tranquil valleys, and bathed in the rejuvenating waters of a waterfall. Climbing to the summit, I became one with the breathtaking views of creation. It was an exhaustive, yet exhilarating day, and now, I am finally at rest, relishing the magnificence of my freedom.

Around the fire, a holy fire, I close my eyes and surrender to the stillness. I begin to let go, allowing my spirit to be free, rest, and soar. I am absorbed into the warmth of the flames. I am at peace. I am filled with profound gratitude for the fire, the giver of warmth and light, whose essence comforts me, body, mind, and spirit. The sound of the crackling wood, the aroma of the smoke, and the radiance of the light all awaken my senses, and I receive them as sacred offerings.

I express my heartfelt thanks to the fire for its gifts. It is a source of shelter and security, imparting comfort out in the middle of nowhere. I am at peace, joyful, and fulfilled. Suddenly, my mind awakens to reality. I see the attribute of fire as the essence of Zen. Its smoke, heat, light, and solace are Zen.

I look deep into the fire. I see the source. Jesus is the fire.

The fire creates the essence of everything I experience. Jesus is the Tree of Life, the giver of grace, the eternal source of everything good, and I am in His presence. Everything Jesus is Beatitude. I am blessed.

******

Beatitude Code: The harmony of body, mind, and spirit is discovered within the peace of Christ.

Lectio Divina: *In the beginning was the Word, and the Word was with God, and the Word was God.* John 1:1 (NIV)

Chapter Eleven

LIGHT OF THE WORLD

He has shown you, O mortal, what is good.
And what does the Lord require of you? To act justly and to love
mercy and to walk humbly with your God.
Micah 6:8 (NIV)

Blessed are the Merciful

A s Jesus wiped His brow, He was aware that some might mis-understand the next Beatitude as simply performing acts of mercy rather than embodying the essence of mercy itself. For Jesus, becoming merciful was more than just doing something; it was about being something.

With prayerful intention, He said, "Blessed are the merciful, for they shall obtain mercy." Jesus understood that by leading a life marked by mercy and compassion, individuals not only gained mercy themselves but also rose above the constraints of judgment.

Jesus reminds us that an eye-for-an-eye attitude means the whole world goes blind. As a kid on the playground, I quickly learned to stand up for myself. My dad taught me most bullies back down when confronted. And I discovered if you are being fair and right-minded, it usually works until you get a black eye. I was not a bully and sought friendship first. I have had a few black eyes, but I have always had good friends. As we age, the playground gets more sophisticated, less honest, and sometimes downright ugly. We take our hurts, disappointments, and betrayals out in various ways, from self-destructive behaviors to backbiting, gossip, and sabotage.

Jesus is discussing the profound concept of radical compassion and mercy that aligns with the very essence of God's heart. As beings made in the image of God, we are summoned to emulate Jesus in every aspect of our lives. Jesus consistently extended mercy to the marginalized and those who may not have appeared deserving. Mercy, at its core, is a state of the heart that ultimately paves the way for forgiveness and compassion.

Mercy is more than good intentions. It demands complete engagement. In the same vein, mercy is not devoid of discernment. Jesus instructs us that mercy is not merely an action but an attitude and a way of life.

The Beatitude of Mercy emphasizes the opportunity for redemption, highlighting that regardless of our past sins or failures, we can always turn to God and experience His boundless mercy. By extending mercy to others, we create a channel to receive that same mercy. The Beatitude of Mercy promises that we receive God's mercy when we go beyond good intentions and freely give mercy to others.

Mercy is a Picture of the Heart

> *There is no fear in love. But perfect love drives out fear,*
> *because fear has to do with punishment.*
> *The one who fears is not made perfect in love.*
> 1 John 4:18 (NIV)

Fear stifles the expression of mercy, choking the potency of love in our relationships with both others and God. It occupies significant mental and emotional real estate, leaving limited room for the presence of God and meaningful connections with others.

When consumed by fear, we tend to hold onto grudges, judge harshly, or withhold forgiveness because we fear being hurt, taken advantage of, or deceived again. We may fear that if we extend mercy to someone who has wronged us, they might not change or appreciate our kindness, and we could be hurt again. Unchecked fear can manifest itself in situations that may have not even happened. We project our fear into future situations.

Sadly, when we project our fear, we tend to withdraw from relationships that might be meaningful and fulfilling. We also cannot be instruments of God's peace and imitate the mercy of Jesus to those who might need us. Some people believe they are merciful because of their acts of mercy. Acts of mercy are good. They help others, and we usually get the recognition. But Jesus is talking about a heart of mercy that hears the heartbeat of God, finding satisfaction in the mercy it receives and gives freely.

Forgiveness is the Core

Forgiveness is the fire that forges the heart of mercy. It forms the foundational strength upon which mercy can be built, layer upon layer, in a continuous cycle of compassion. Compassion, in this context, means not only feeling empathy or sympathy for others but also actively responding to their needs with kindness, understanding, and forgiveness. It involves going beyond mere feelings of pity to take action to alleviate suffering, offer support, or extend forgiveness and understanding, even to those who may not seem deserving.

A Gift to Ourselves

Behold Jesus upon the cross—bruised, shamed, ridiculed, and innocent. Yet, from His lips emerges the profound plea, *"Father, forgive them, for they know not what they do"* (Luke 23:34 ESV). Whenever we feel betrayed or disappointed by someone, it helps to recall the image of Jesus on that cross. It serves as a poignant reminder that our grievances, though valid, pale in comparison. Even in our moments of anger, frustration, and confusion, we are reminded of God's call to extend forgiveness.

At times, the prospect of forgiving may seem insurmountable. But now, armed with a deeper understanding of the Beatitudes, failing to forgive would only diminish the mercy within us. To manifest the profound mercy that Jesus emphasizes, it is imperative to wholeheartedly embrace the practice of forgiveness, especially when it appears most daunting. This is precisely why, within the Divine progression of the Beatitudes, we first learn to mourn. It is through mourning that we learn the vital lesson of being unreservedly honest with God, a crucial step in the process of forgiving those who have caused us pain. Forgiveness implies there is a deep pain within.

When we withhold forgiveness from others, we fall short of demonstrating mercy, and our hearts and attitudes remain distant from the essence of the heart of mercy Jesus is teaching us.

Isn't it interesting how the church dedicates so much time to claiming the forgiveness of Jesus, but spends so little time teaching us the value of forgiving others or how to? Yet we instinctively know that a person who harbors unforgiveness becomes a prisoner of their unforgiveness.

Anger

Jesus got angry at the business community of his day for taking advantage of the poor in the temple. You could even say it was an act of mercy. Anger, often maligned as a purely negative emotion, holds a critical place in the tapestry of human feelings and mercy. Anger when wielded wisely, serves as a vigilant guardian of our integrity and the well-being of those around us. It prompts us to establish and uphold the limits that protect us from harm and disrespect, ensuring that our personal space and dignity are maintained.

However, the beneficial aspects of anger are highly dependent on its management. When anger lingers beyond its useful life—when it overstays its welcome—it morphs into a source of destruction. It turns inward, breeding resentment, or outward, fostering conflict and alienation. Anger that becomes chronic or unyielding often loses its initial protective purpose, veering into the territory of self-sabotage and egotism. It's when we cling to anger, allowing it to dominate our thoughts and actions, that it becomes a barrier to personal growth and healthy relationships.

Yet, when recognized and expressed consciously, anger can be profoundly transformative. It acts as a beacon to consciousness where boundaries have been breached and where attention is needed. This visible, palpable form of anger is a gift, illuminating the contours of our identity and the parameters within which we seek to interact with the world. It guides us in understanding not only our limits but also the extent of our empathy towards the hurt and alienation experienced by others.

Conscious anger, therefore, plays a pivotal role in self-discovery and communal harmony. It teaches us about the depths of our convictions and the values we are unwilling to compromise. Moreover, it helps us navigate the complex web of human relationships, signaling when to stand firm, when to negotiate, and when to extend our understanding and compassion. In essence, anger, when acknowledged and harnessed as a force for good, becomes an indispensable tool in the ongoing task of defining who we are, what we stand for, and how we relate to the world around us. It is through this lens that we can appreciate anger not as an enemy, but as a powerful ally in the quest for self-awareness and for extending mercy.

A key impediment to embodying the Beatitude of Mercy lies in our often-unconscious failure to acknowledge the anger within us. This oversight is not merely about overlooking a fleeting feeling of irritation; it's about failing to confront a deeper, more pervasive emotion that can color our perceptions and interactions. Anger, in its many forms, can be a significant barrier to practicing mercy. It can harden our hearts and blind us to the needs and sufferings of others, making it challenging to extend compassion or forgiveness.

To truly exercise mercy, as extolled in the Beatitudes, it is imperative to embark on a journey of self-awareness. This involves a deliberate introspection to recognize and understand the sources of our anger—be it unresolved personal grievances, feelings of injustice, or even deeper psychological wounds. Recognizing our anger requires honesty and vulnerability, as it compels us to face aspects of ourselves that we may prefer to ignore or suppress.

Furthermore, this process of recognition is not an end but a crucial step towards transformation. By acknowledging our anger, we can begin to work through it, seeking healing and reconciliation with ourselves and others. This path allows us to soften our hearts and open ourselves up to the possibility of mercy. It is through this transformation that we can genuinely embody the Beatitude of Mercy, extending kindness, forgiveness, and compassion to those around us, even in the face of personal grievances or societal injustices.

In essence, the failure to exercise mercy often stems from an unrecognized anger within us. Overcoming this barrier requires a deep and honest reflection on our emotional state, followed by a conscious effort to heal and reconcile these feelings. Only then can we truly live out the Beatitude of Mercy, fostering a more compassionate and forgiving world.

The Divine Sequence

Forgiveness is a gift we give ourselves, and the blessing of the Beatitudes is we shall likewise receive mercy. After Jesus delivered the Beatitudes, He immediately returned to forgiveness, saying, *"For if you forgive other people when they sin against you, your heavenly Father will also forgive you. But if you do not forgive others their sins, your Father will not forgive your sins"* (Matt. 6:14-15 NIV).

When Jesus was asked what the greatest commandment was, He answered, *"'Love the Lord your God with all your heart and with all your soul and with all your mind and with all your strength.' The second is: 'Love your neighbor as yourself.' There is no commandment greater than these"* (Mark 12:30-31 NIV). This is the worldview Jesus gives to us. Jesus serves as the living embodiment of love, illustrating the essence of love through the boundless mercy He extended to others and the mercy that God bestows upon us, as exemplified through His sacrificial act on the cross.

It occurs organically. The deeper you immerse yourself in the presence of the Christ Spirit, the clearer it becomes that the essence of our belief centers around forgiveness. This is where the transformation of our faith gets its wings and begins to soar.

In the Divine sequence of the Beatitudes, mercy comes in the middle. We are reborn in Christ so we can grow up in Christ. At first, infants are unknowingly self-centered because they are preoccupied with their own needs and desires. Much like babies who cry out, "Feed me, change my diapers, hold me, let me sleep, play with me," this spiritual rebirth represents a turning point in our faith journey – but it's just the beginning. As we mature in Christ, we learn to be less self-centered. As we become poor in spirit, mourn, and meek, we grow into becoming merciful.

In the renowned "love chapter," the apostle Paul highlights the three most significant attributes of following Jesus: faith, hope, and love, underscoring that the greatest among these is love. Furthermore, in this passage, Paul imparts a profound truth, stating, *"When I was a child, I spoke as a child, I understood as a child, I thought as a child; but when I became a man, I put away childish things"* (1 Cor.13:11 NIV).

To paraphrase my college pastor, Dr. Ed Young, during a sermon, he said we can be mature at nineteen or seventy in Christ, or we can be Christian our entire lives and remain a baby. We're still in Christ, we just never grew up.

Paul's message resonates with Christians as a call to mature in their faith, cultivating attributes like faith, hope, and love. This signifies a transition from a self-centered perspective (characteristic of infancy) to a more selfless and Christ-centered life.

On the journey of the Beatitudes, we are continually maturing, moving beyond the "me, me, me" mentality. As highlighted in Rich

Warren's book, *The Purpose Driven Life*, the opening sentence poignantly states, "It's not about you."[13] True authenticity, spiritual maturity in Christ, and personal fulfillment stem from aligning with God's purpose for our lives.

Among the most profound attributes one can possess is that of being merciful. It reflects a growing relationship with the Holy Spirit and the will to follow the teachings of Jesus, witnessed by our willingness to extend compassion and forgiveness to others.

In the middle of the Sermon on the Mount, Jesus teaches us how to pray. Notice that forgiveness lies at the center of His thoughts:

> *Our Father, which art in heaven,*
> *Hallowed be thy name.*
> *Thy kingdom come,*
> *Thy will be done on earth,*
> *As it is in heaven.*
> *Give us this day our daily bread.*
> *And forgive us our debts,*
> *As we forgive our debtors.*
> *And lead us not into temptation,*
> *But deliver us from evil:*
> *For thine is the kingdom,*
> *And the power and the glory,*
> *For ever Amen.*
> Matthew 6:9-13 (KJV)

Forgive and Bless

My wife and I attended a marriage seminar at The Church of the Highlands in Birmingham, Alabama, at the invitation of our daughter, Shelli, and her husband, Mike. One of the most spiritually impactful moments of my life occurred during this event when the speaker asked everyone to stand and forgive those they needed to forgive in their lives. He allowed ample time (ten minutes or more) for this process. As my wife and I stood up, a serendipitous gust from the air conditioner above sent shivers down our spines, signifying the presence of the Holy Spirit (God has a sense of humor).

The experience was profoundly moving. In the subsequent session, the speaker had us stand once more and silently offer prayers of blessing for those we had forgiven. This newfound freedom allowed us to shed burdens, soften our hearts, and create space for Jesus in our souls, making it an incredible and transformative experience.

The ABCs

Listening to the radio on my drive home to finish this chapter, I tuned in to Dr. Dobson's show. His guest was author and theologian Dr. R.T. Kendall. They were talking about forgiveness, exactly what I had planned to write on to finish this section on mercy (another Godwink). Dr. Kendall had just published a book called *Total Forgiveness*. He used the story of Joseph to explain how the Christ Spirit taught Joseph how to live by forgiving his brothers who sold him into slavery.

This is a brief outline of what Dr. Rendall learned and talked about. While I had come to appreciate many of the same principles of forgiveness he talked about, I was blown away by how pragmatic his advice was:

- When you forgive someone, do not tell anyone else what they have done to harm you. The exception is a confidential conversation with a mentor, pastor, mate, parent, or counselor.
- Don't let the person you have been wronged by become afraid of you because of your attitude, anger, hurt, or frustrations.
- Don't make the people who have hurt you and who you need to forgive feel guilty. Scripture says that's God's role, not ours.
- Allow the people you need to forgive to save face. Always treat them with dignity and give them a backdoor to escape respectfully. Putting someone down or backing them into a corner will

only exacerbate the situation, and that means you never really forgave them.

- Protect the people you need to forgive by not sharing their darkest secrets or fears you have become aware of. We tend to spread the bad things about people who have hurt us. This keeps the cycle of hurt in motion. Forgive and choose to forget. This does not mean you are not aware.
- Forgiving is a life sentence. As soon as you forgive, your hurt will try to resurface because you are human, and you need to keep forgiving. Pray for them daily and pray for blessings in their lives.
- Accept that the situation might never get better, but you will.[14]

Forgiveness is not how the people respond to you. It's all on you, and without God, it is impossible. These principles take grace to accept. Forgiveness takes practice, practice, and practice to become part of who you are in Christ.

Practicing Mercy

I learned many of these principles early in my career as director of social work for the Masonic Children's Home. As newlyweds, my wife and I were thrown in the middle of the lives of ninety-nine children whose backgrounds were troublesome. One of my jobs was dealing with their parents, who were unable to function as healthy parents and productive citizens.

Mr. Hamrick, our superintendent, imparted a crucial lesson to me. He taught me the importance of consistently extending dignity to everyone, even those who were very challenging individuals (e.g., drunks, drug addicts, prostitutes, abusive parents, etc.) while maintaining a steadfast commitment to prioritizing the well-being of their children, regardless of their words or actions.

This was a daunting task of navigating incredibly challenging situations, which often involved enduring insults, shouting, and verbal abuse from parents. During these trying times, Mr. Hamrick imparted a Christ-centered lesson on how to handle such confrontations.

When the children's parents became unruly, Mr. Hamrick advised me to maintain my composure, express appreciation for their visit, and suggest we could meet again the next day once they had had a chance to calm down. Remarkably, in every instance, they promptly apologized and expressed their willingness to continue the conversation. The underlying principle was to return the next day, ensuring that they treated me with the same respect I was extending to them. This approach emphasized that forgiveness is rooted in perspective and unchecked emotions can weaken its transformative power.

On those difficult days, as soon as they left my office, it was a relief. Somehow, I needed to pray to forgive them so I could be a blessing, not a hindrance. Eventually, with God's forgiveness looming over us, we forged many good relationships and found effective therapies for the children and their parents. In a way, I had become an instrument of God's mercy with the leadership of Mr. Hamrick.

Forgiveness is the key that unlocks the code, *"Blessed are the merciful, for they shall receive mercy."* Once followers of Jesus embrace mercy and forgiveness, the wheels of faith begin to roll.

Words Matter

Your words matter. At the time of Jesus, there were a couple of Jewish idioms that can, if we understand them, help us to see Scripture and the Beatitudes through the eyes of Jesus. Words play a big role in developing a merciful heart.

"Motzeh shem ra" refers to the act of tarnishing someone's reputation by spreading falsehoods or engaging in slander. Left unaddressed, motzeh shem ra can become a persistent and damaging pattern within relationships. During the time of Jesus, these very words were employed to characterize leprosy, an affliction that gradually eroded a person's well-being from the inside out.

"**Lashon hara**" doesn't involve fabricating falsehoods. Instead, it manifests as a passive-aggressive behavior where we employ negative truths to harm others while seemingly expressing concern. This behavior can become a persistent and infectious pattern, causing a rift between one's physical, mental, and spiritual well-being, thereby keeping the peace of Christ at a distance.

The prophetic cadence of the Beatitudes guides us through the initial steps of being "poor in spirit" and mourning. This journey encourages us to welcome the presence of the Holy Spirit into our lives and confront our sins with unflinching candor, mourning them for the sake of our healing. As we wholeheartedly commit to the process of nurturing a state of humility, mourning, and earnestly seeking God's will, we come to recognize our profound need for God's mercy—to receive it and give it away.

At times, we perceive mercy as something we can control, like a faucet we can open and close. However, the mercy that Jesus speaks of is like a continuous river, seamlessly becoming a part of who we are.

The Power of Words

The following passages emphasize the importance of the words we choose:

- **Proverbs 18:21 (NIV):** *The tongue has the power of life and death, and those who love it will eat its fruit.* This verse emphasizes the significant impact our words can have on others.
- **Ephesians 4:29 (NIV):** *Do not let any unwholesome talk come out of your mouths, but only what helps build others up according to their needs, that it may benefit those who listen.*

This verse encourages believers to use their words for edification and encouragement rather than negativity.

- **James 3:5-6 (NIV):** *Likewise, the tongue is a small part of the body, but it makes great boasts. Consider what a great forest is set on fire by a small spark. The tongue also is a fire, a world of evil among the parts of the body. It corrupts the whole body, sets the whole course of one's life on fire, and is itself set on fire by hell.* This passage warns about the potential destructiveness of our words.
- **Colossians 4:6 (NIV):** *Let your conversation be always full of grace, seasoned with salt, so that you may know how to answer everyone.* Here, believers are encouraged to speak with grace and wisdom in their interactions with others.
- **Matthew 12:36-37 (NIV):** *But I tell you that everyone will have to give account on the day of judgment for every empty word they have spoken. For by your words, you will be acquitted, and by your words, you will be condemned.* These verses underscore the accountability for our words and their significance.

Our readiness to forgive and the language we use brings power to the truth, *"Blessed are the merciful, for they will receive mercy."*

****

Beatitude Code: Forgiveness is a gift we give ourselves. It is "The Way" we follow Jesus.

Lectio Divina: *Then Peter came up and said to him, "Lord, how often will my brother sin against me, and I forgive him? As many as seven times?" Jesus said to him, "I do not say to you seven times, but seventy-seven times."* Matthew 18:21-22 (ESV)

Chapter Twelve

SEEKING AN OASIS

"We need to find God, and he cannot be found in noise and restless-ness. God is the friend of silence. See how nature—trees, flowers, grass—grow in silence; see the stars, the moon and the sun, how they move in silence. We need silence to be to touch souls."
Mother Teresa

Blessed are Those Who Hunger and Thirst for Righteousness

As Jesus stood on the gentle slope overlooking the gathered crowd, a sense of profound purpose filled the air around Him. The azure sky stretched infinitely above; a canvas painted with the hues of Divine inspiration.

In that moment, Jesus was about to challenge the very essence of conventional religious wisdom. The crowds, who had long been immersed in the teachings of established faiths, gathered before Him, their hearts heavy with the weight of centuries-old doctrines. The prevailing dogma preached righteousness as a lofty ideal, an unattainable pinnacle, an elusive dream forever out of reach. It was a prescription for guilt, a never-ending journey to grasp a perfection they could never truly attain.

With a calm and steady demeanor, Jesus was about to unveil a revelation that would rattle the foundations of religious tradition. *"Blessed are those who hunger and thirst for righteousness,"* He began, His voice resonating like the tranquil ripple of a clear mountain stream, *"for they shall be satisfied."*

As these words hung in the air, they created ripples of astonishment among His listeners. Here was a revolutionary message, a radical shift in perspective. Jesus was not advocating for righteousness as an attainable goal. He proclaimed it as a path, an ongoing journey, that led to fulfillment, not frustration.

At that moment, the listeners were transported to a realm where religious norms were rewritten. They saw, with their hearts, that it was the yearning for righteousness, the hunger and thirst for a better, more just world, that was the true essence of spirituality. It was not about conforming to an unattainable standard but embracing a relentless pursuit of what was right and just—a tireless quest for justice.

Jesus, the gentle rebel, had turned the religious paradigm on its head. Deep within His being, He knew that the thirst for righteousness was not a futile endeavor, but a wellspring of Divine grace. In a world weighed down by the oppressive burdens of religious legalism, He offered a beacon of hope, a path that was both profound and simple— the path to righteousness was to seek it, not obtain it. When Jesus spoke these words, He knew the path He was walking was straight to a cross where His righteousness would more than make up for what we could not obtain without Him.

In essence, Jesus is saying to "hunger and thirst for righteousness" by following Him. Give up on the noun of righteousness. Be the verb seeking righteousness.

The God Thing

Within the sacred Scriptures, the terms "righteous" and "righteousness" grace its pages a remarkable 613 times. In the rich mosaic of Judeo-Christian theology, righteousness emerges as a concept profoundly woven into the fabric of faith. It is a notion of moral and ethical purity, an unwavering uprightness that resonates in harmony with the Divine standards and commandments set forth by God.

When Jesus proclaimed, *"Blessed are those who hunger and thirst for righteousness, for they will be satisfied,"* He was, indeed, elevating the concept of righteousness beyond a mere adherence to the Ten Commandments. And Jesus was quick to say he did not come to abolish the Ten Commandments but to fulfill them. He was emphasizing the transformation of the human heart into one that passionately seeks to enact justice for the glory of God. This profound teaching finds validation throughout the Scriptures.

- **Isaiah 64:6 (NIV)**: *"All of us have become like one who is unclean, and all our righteous acts are like filthy rags."* This verse from the Old Testament highlights the inadequacy of human attempts to attain righteousness on their own. It underscores the need for a deeper, God-centered understanding of righteousness.
- **Romans 3:10 (NIV)**: *As it is written: "There is no one righteous, not even one."* This verse from the New Testament reinforces the idea that righteousness is not something that cannot be achieved by human effort alone but is found in following the path of Jesus, who is righteous.
- **Matthew 5:20 (ESV)**: *"For I tell you, unless your righteousness exceeds that of the scribes and Pharisees, you will never enter the kingdom of heaven."* Here, Jesus challenges His followers to move beyond a superficial adherence to the law (as exhibited by the Pharisees) and to seek a righteousness that goes deeper, one that aligns with the heart and character of Christ.
- **Matthew 6:33 (ESV)**: *"But seek first the kingdom of God and his righteousness, and all these things will be added to you."* This verse underscores the importance of prioritizing God's righteousness above all else and seeking it as a primary pursuit in life.

By emphasizing a hunger and thirst for righteousness, Jesus encouraged His followers to cultivate a deep, passionate desire to see justice and righteousness through the eyes of Christ, not through their limited perspective. It's an invitation to align one's heart with the heart of God, recognizing that true righteousness comes not from outward adherence to rules but from a genuine transformation of the inner self, following the character of Christ. It's a call to actively seek God's justice and righteousness in the world, knowing that through this pursuit, they will find the true satisfaction that comes from living in harmony with God's will.

The God Flow

Think of faith as embarking on a river rafting expedition. In this spiritual voyage down the river's path, you encounter different dimensions of the faith journey. There are peaceful stretches where your advancement is gentle, allowing for moments of tranquil reflection. Thrilling rapids emerge, injecting excitement into your odyssey, interspersed with moments of warmth as you bask in the sun's embrace, occasionally refreshed by invigorating splashes of water. Yet there are also instances when you come across stagnant pools that abruptly impede your raft's progress. During these times, the incessant chatter of your mind disrupts the aspirations of your spirit, attempting to seize control.

Often, your thoughts fixate on the money you've contributed, the assistance you've extended to others, the earnest prayers you've offered, the unwavering commitment you've demonstrated, your diligent study of Scripture, and your consistent participation in the church community. These thoughts may adopt a dualistic quality, subtly leading you to believe that you possess inherent virtue and, perhaps, even making you feel superior to others. In these moments of quiet contemplation, the seeds of self-righteousness discover fertile ground to establish themselves.

Nonetheless, it is crucial to remember that much like a river that flows continuously, your faith should maintain its fluidity and humility. It requires vigilance against the allure of self-righteousness that may emerge during these moments of stagnation. Rather, persist in navigating the river of faith with humility, recognizing that your righteousness emanates from the source of God's grace rather than from your actions. By doing so, you can avoid these stagnant pools and enable your faith to thrive and evolve as you continue your spiritual voyage.

RIGHTEOUSNESS

What does righteousness look like? Job describes it best: *"I put on righteousness as my clothing; justice was my robe and my turban. I was eyes to the blind and feet to the lame. I was a father to the needy; I took up the case of the stranger. I broke the fangs of the wicked and snatched the victims from their teeth."* Job 29:14-17 (NIV)

Our existence, composed of the mind, body, and spirit, constitutes the core of our soul. Within this soul, the condition of our heart holds paramount importance. In numerous scriptural references, the heart is prominently featured. For the Hebrews, the heart encompassed not only their emotions but also their thoughts, words, and deeds, all guided by the mind's intentions. This distinction is vital as it highlights our capacity to distort the concept of righteousness to align with our ego-driven desires or, even worse, we become indifferent.

However, authentic transformation through Christ, directed toward serving the kingdom of God in the present moment, requires an active and dynamic perspective. It is a perspective that flows freely rather than remaining stagnant, enabling us to align our hearts, minds, words, and actions with the Divine will rather than our self-serving Inclinations.

In essence, Job's description of righteousness paints a comprehensive picture of a person who is morally upright and actively engaged in acts of kindness, justice, and compassion. It is a way of living and seeing life that extends beyond one's benefit and extends a helping hand to those in need while steadfastly opposing injustice. Job's words are a timeless reminder that we live blessed in the presence of the Lord, which provides the energy and inspiration to seek righteousness *"on earth as it is in heaven"* (Matt. 6:10).

Righteousness is not a self-aggrandizing state but a profound spiritual condition where we find blessings, contentment, and fulfillment through our service to God and His kingdom. Instead of elevating ourselves as self-righteous individuals, we view ourselves as channels of flowing water dedicated to serving God and advancing His Divine purpose. By adopting this perspective, we become vessels of His grace, constantly replenished, and illuminated by the Salvation that flows through us.

Fruits Of The Spirit

"Blessed are those who thirst and hunger for righteousness, for they shall be filled" beautifully complements what the apostle Paul wrote about receiving the fruit of the Spirit.

In Galatians 5:22-23, Paul described the fruit of the Spirit as love, joy, peace, patience, kindness, goodness, faithfulness, gentleness, and self-control. This passage highlights the transformative work of the Holy Spirit within believers, producing these qualities in their lives. These qualities are God's way of fulfilling us. It is enough.

The connection between Jesus's statement and Paul's teaching lies in the reality that those who hunger and thirst for righteousness are the individuals who open themselves to the work of the Holy Spirit. When we earnestly desire righteousness, we invite the Spirit's presence and guidance into our lives.

As we seek righteousness with a fervent heart, the Spirit works within us, producing the fruit of love, joy, peace, and all the other virtues listed by Paul. This process of seeking righteousness and bearing the fruit of the Spirit leads to a life filled with spiritual abundance and reflects the character of Christ. To be blessed, remember is, when Yahweh's presence is increased in your life.

The desire to seek righteousness springs from our spirit's intuition and consciousness to seek Jesus in everything. We were created to be seekers, and we all seek something; it's a matter of what or who we seek.

Righteousness is something we seek, not who we are.

****

Beatitude Code: The hunger and thirst for righteousness is the alchemy of the Holy Spirit.

Lectio Divina: *"So I say, walk by the Spirit, and you will not gratify the desires of the flesh. For the flesh desires what is contrary to the Spirit, and the Spirit what is contrary to the flesh. They are in conflict with each other, so that you are not to do whatever you want. But if you are led by the Spirit, you are not under the law. The acts of the flesh are obvious: sexual immorality, impurity and debauchery; idolatry and witchcraft; hatred, discord, jealousy, fits of rage, selfish ambition, dissensions, factions and envy; drunkenness, orgies, and the like. I warn you, as I did before, that those who live like this will not inherit the kingdom of God. But the fruit of the Spirit is love, joy, peace, forbearance, kindness, goodness, faithfulness, gentleness and self-control. Against such things there is no law. Those who belong to Christ Jesus have crucified the flesh with its passions and desires. Since we live by the Spirit, let us keep in step with the Spirit. Let us not become conceited, provoking and envying each other."* Galatians 5:16-26 (NIV)

Chapter Thirteen

TRANSCENDENTAL JOURNEY

Create in me a pure heart, O God,
and renew a steadfast spirit within me.
Psalm 51:10

Blessed are the Pure in Heart, for They Shall See God

As the sun set over the horizon, a hush fell over the crowd gathered before Jesus. They watched in wonder as He again paused, His eyes closed in contemplation, before delivering the words that would echo through the ages.

"Blessed are the pure in heart," He began, His voice soft yet commanding. The gentle breeze lifted His gaze toward heaven, and the warm glow of the setting sun illuminated His face, casting it in a golden light.

"For they shall see God," He finished, His words ringing like a bell in the stillness of the setting sun. The assembled crowd held their breath as they heard "The pure in heart will see God." They had been told their entire lives if they saw God that they would surely die. If it had been anyone other than Jesus, they would have gotten up and left. Jesus, however, taught with authority from heaven and they listened.

At that moment, it seemed as if time stood still, and all that existed was the figure of Jesus. His words hung in the air like a sweet melody lingering long after it had been played. The disciples took a deep breath, feeling the weight of those words, while at the exact moment, it filled their hearts. Something was changing, perhaps their hearts, for they were seeing the son of God.

Why is it that some people in the presence of Jesus see him for who He is, and others never see Him at all?

A Pure Heart

As I initially contemplated the parable of a pure heart, I believed I possessed a good heart, a kind heart, an understanding heart, and even an open-minded heart. I questioned whether these qualities somehow converge like streams into a river, forming a pure heart.

I thought the blessing of this Beatitude must be like the other Beatitude blessings, like the promise of the kingdom of heaven when one is poor in spirit. That is when the lights came on. I realized all the blessings, including the kingdom of heaven, were as much about the here and now as the afterlife. Therefore, this would mean the blessing of a pure heart is seeing God *in the here and now.*

How is this possible? Even Moses, when in the presence of the burning bush, had to avert his gaze. The audience to whom Jesus spoke was aware of this. What exactly was Jesus saying? Then, prayerfully, I remembered a story I had heard my entire life. When Jesus was crucified, the temple's veil was torn in two. This veil had separated the rest of the temple from the Holy of Holies, where God dwelled. During a specific ritual once a year, the high priest would enter the Holy of Holies. They even tied a rope to the high priest's leg in case he encountered God and perished, allowing them to pull him out.

Upon realizing that the temple's veil was torn in half, a revelation dawned on me as bright as a beam of light. It became evident that the blessings of a pure heart reached their zenith when all the preceding Beatitudes converged in perfect harmony, forming the spear's tip of spiritual transformation. A pure heart transcends a mere belief system. It is an intrinsic facet of becoming a Christlike individual, a natural extension of who Elohim created us to be. By embodying this transformation, we embark on a journey to behold the countenance of El Shaddai, not solely in the afterlife, but woven into the very fabric of our present life experiences.

Here lies the irony, the curious turn of this specific paradox: A pure heart isn't something we own; it is the very blessing itself, the ability to behold the face of God. The paradox of a pure heart brings to life the interdependence of all the Beatitudes. This understanding propels us further into the enlightenment of our salvation.

As a result, we become acutely aware of God's presence permeating everything. We discern the reflection of being created in God's image within every individual. This awakening prompts us to abandon judgment and, instead, extend forgiveness, mirroring God's own forgiveness toward us.

We start to perceive the interconnectedness of "everything Jesus" in the realms of the physical, the intellectual, and the spiritual. As we grow more Christlike, we find ourselves in the presence of God, allowing us to glimpse God's countenance beyond the limitations of our ego.

The presence of God is everywhere. We know this theology, but do we live it? When engaging with individuals who dedicate their time to working in homeless shelters, they often express how they readily discern the face of God in the countenances of the homeless.

Rabbi – Teacher

Receiving a pure heart, as Jesus speaks of in the Beatitudes, involves a transformative journey of spiritual growth. Here are some key teachings and steps from Jesus Himself:

- **Repentance and Forgiveness**: In the Gospel of Matthew, Jesus teaches that if you are offering your gift at the altar and remember that your brother or sister has something against you, leave your gift there and first go and be reconciled to them, then come and offer your gift (Matt. 5:23-24). This emphasizes the importance of forgiveness and reconciliation as steps toward purity of heart. To have a pure heart, one must let go of grudges, anger, and resentment and seek forgiveness and reconciliation with others.

- **Love and Compassion:** In Matthew 22:37-39, Jesus instructs us to love the Lord our God with all our heart, soul, and mind and to love our neighbor as ourselves. Practicing love and compassion toward others is a way to purify the heart. Jesus often demonstrated compassion and urged His followers to do the same, emphasizing the importance of selflessness and empathy.

- **Humility:** Jesus frequently spoke about humility. In Matthew 18:3-4 (NIV), He says, *"Truly I tell you, unless you change and become like little children, you will never enter the kingdom of heaven. Therefore, whoever takes the lowly position of this child is the greatest in the kingdom of heaven."* Cultivating humility involves recognizing our need for God's grace and acknowledging that we are not self-sufficient. A pure heart is open to God's transformative work within and transcendent purpose.

- **Purity of Intentions:** In Matthew 6:22 (NIV), Jesus says, *"The eye is the lamp of the body. If your eyes are healthy, your whole body will be full of light."* This verse underscores the importance of having pure intentions and motives. Selfish desires or hidden agendas do not drive a pure heart. A pure heart is consistently in fellowship with the Christ Spirit, and being in His presence is purifying, not by actions but singularly by the presence of the Holiest of Holies.

- **Seeking God's Kingdom:** In Matthew 6:33 (NIV), Jesus teaches, *"But seek first his kingdom and his righteousness, and all these things will be given to you as well."* Prioritizing God's kingdom above worldly pursuits and desires is essential for purifying the heart. It involves seeking God's will, righteousness, and the values of His kingdom above all else. God's kingdom becomes our primary world view.

- **Prayer and Relationship with God:** Throughout His ministry, Jesus emphasized the significance of prayer and maintaining a close relationship with God. In the Sermon on the Mount, He instructs His followers to pray secretly and commune with God in the inner chambers of their hearts (Matt. 6:6). Such communion with God through prayer fosters a pure heart by allowing God's presence to transform and cleanse it.

When discussing the interconnectedness of God, it's crucial to bear in mind that the love of God is inscribed within our hearts. God's essence is woven into the fabric of creation all around us. Scripture serves as the Living Word of God. Moreover, before His ascension, Jesus pledged to send His Holy Spirit to be with us. As we embark on our individual faith journeys, we effectively become the eyes, ears, hands, and feet of Christ in this world.

The Incarnate Christ

Christ is perpetually present, always seeking a place within our hearts.

Now, Christ speaks through the voices and eyes of ordinary people, such as factory workers, retail clerks, executives, professors, beggars, waiters, and children. He extends His eyes so we can see the Divine rhythms pulsating around us. He walks alongside us through the feet of soldiers and the homeless, and in the hearts of those in need, He yearns for refuge. Offering shelter or food to anyone who asks or needs it is offering it to Christ.

However, it's important to acknowledge that it's not always easy to remember this profound truth: If every person was exceptionally holy and radiated the presence of "another Christ," it would be effortless to recognize Christ in everyone.

Consider this. Had Mary arrived in Bethlehem riding on a chariot, free from the weariness of a day's dusty and sweltering journey, wearing an impressive array of jewels, such as diamonds, sapphires, and emeralds, and accompanied by a retinue of servants at her every whim, undoubtedly, people would have readily found her a room at the inn? But God chose a different path. Even Christ on the cross could have summoned a legion of angels to save Him, but He did not.

In the life of Jesus, there were always a few who made up those who could not see God's face in the ordinary. The shepherds did it. They hurried to the crib to atone for people caught up in their indifference. The wise men did it. They journeyed across the world to make up for those who refused to disrupt the routines of their lives to go to Christ.

Even the gifts the wise men brought had an obscure benefit for what would follow later in this Child's life. They brought gold, the king's wealth, to make up for the crown of thorns that He would wear. They offered incense, the symbol of joy, to make up for the mockery. The Roman soldiers spit on His face and mocked Him as the "King of the Jews." They gave Him myrrh to heal and soothe. Mel Gibson's movie *The Passion* is hard to watch because it paints a realistic picture of the torture Jesus endured. But Mary, other women, and John were there.

We can be there, too. It's not too late. We can see Christ in friends and strangers, in everyone we encounter. We do not see this as a religious duty—that is always the ego. It always seeks the attention and approval of others. No, our motive is to please Christ. The satisfaction is within our hearts. If God is satisfied, we are satisfied. Those who see the face of God have pure hearts.

If you desire a pure heart, now is an opportune moment to pause, engage in a heartfelt conversation with God, and seek the grace required to receive His presence in the ordinary. We receive grace and do not seize it. The act of receiving grace implies humility and open-ness. It requires acknowledging one's need for God and one's inability to achieve salvation or spiritual growth through one's own efforts. This stance contrasts sharply with the idea of seizing, which implies taking control or claiming something through force or entitlement. Grace, by its nature, cannot be seized because it operates beyond the economy of exchange or the principle of earning.

****

Insight: We follow Jesus wherever we are because that is where we are.

Beatitude Code: God's presence purifies our hearts.

Lectio Divina: *"Delight yourself in the LORD, and he will give you the desires of your heart."* Psalm 37:4 (ESV)

Chapter Fourteen

BRIDGES NOT WALLS

"Darkness cannot drive out darkness: only light can do that.
Hate cannot drive out hate: only love can do that."
Martin Luther King Jr.

Blessed are the Peacemakers

As Jesus stood before the crowd on the hillside, He was acutely aware that His message was far from straightforward. The Beatitudes He articulated carried a profound sense of paradox, and He understood that those who listened would need time to grapple with and contemplate their significance. This truth was as countercultural then as it remains today, challenging conventional wisdom and societal norms.

Jesus recognized that embracing His teachings required patience and commitment. The disciples who accompanied Him during His three-year ministry invested countless hours in His presence, witnessing His actions and absorbing His teachings. Even after His resurrection, they spent another forty days intermittently with Jesus, deepening their understanding of His mission and purpose.

However, it was not until the arrival of the Holy Spirit, as promised by Jesus, that God's redemptive plan came into awareness. At Pentecost, the disciples began to grasp the profound significance of everything Jesus had conveyed and exemplified throughout His life, crucifixion, and resurrection. This revelation marked a transformative moment in their faith journey as the presence of the Holy Spirit enlightened their salvation—as it does ours.

It's essential to remember that this journey began with their courageous decision to follow Jesus. Their willingness to step out in faith and embrace the unconventional teachings of the Messiah ultimately led them to a profound understanding of salvation and the transformative power of Christ's message.

As Jesus looks out over the crowd, He sees the pain, suffering, and division that plagues their lives. He sees the anger and hatred that tears families apart and the violence that destroys communities. But He also sees something else—a glimmer of hope, a spark of Divine love that burns within each person.

Peace and Love

While most of the crowd eagerly anticipated Jesus's words, some regarded His radical message skeptically. Within this diverse assembly, several Roman soldiers stood watch, armed, and prepared to suppress any potential unrest. Additionally, the Jewish leaders were among the onlookers, their gaze fixed intently on Jesus, anticipating any statement they could exploit as a breach of their religious laws.

Jesus's teachings posed a profound threat to the established order of their administrative state. Astonishingly, some individuals were even eager to unearth a religious pretext to justify stoning Him to death. However, amid this palpable tension, Jesus remained remarkably composed and unwavering in His focus.

He understood that His message of peace and love was precisely what the people needed to hear, regardless of the opposition and hostility He encountered. With determination and grace, Jesus remained resolute in sharing this transformative message with those who would listen.

And so, as the crowd hushed to hear His next words, Jesus said in a voice clear and strong, "Blessed are the peacemakers, for they shall be called the children of God."

Children of God

Here it is, my friends. Jesus is bringing us back to who we are. After thousands of years of strife and violence, Jesus wholeheartedly asks us to embrace the Divine purpose of our existence, to discover our identity as children of God—and children of God, we are peacemakers.

****

The last century saw remarkable progress in fields such as technology, healthcare, space exploration, and science. However, this period has also been characterized by extraordinary levels of violence. Conflicts, wars, terrorism, and the adoption of extremist ideologies, including communism and Nazism, have resulted in the loss of hundreds of millions of lives.

****

As children of God, we are peacemakers. If we press into this Beatitude long enough for it to take root, it ignites a spiritual flame within us. The resounding drumbeat of God's boundless love finds its most unmistakable crescendo in the life and ministry of Jesus Christ. He not only proclaimed but personified Divine compassion in ways that left the world astonished. From healing the sick and feeding the hungry to forgiving sins and challenging societal norms, Jesus exemplified love in its purest form. His ultimate act of love on the cross, where He willingly bore the sins of humanity, transcended comprehension, and ushered in a new covenant of grace and reconciliation.

In the Beatitudes, Jesus provides a roadmap for living a life in alignment with God's kingdom. The Beatitude of being a peacemaker underscores the importance of actively fostering peace and reconciliation, mirroring God's nature as a peacemaker. It challenges us to be agents of God's love in a fractured world. We are Divine agents striving for harmony and unity.

What does it take to become a peacemaker? It starts by embodying peace within us and establishing a connection with the wellspring of peace that resides within us. It entails taking a principled stand through nonviolent resistance against unjust systems. Additionally, it requires us to acquire the tools of nonviolent communication and conflict resolution.

Through this Beatitude, Jesus proclaims that God is inherently a peacemaker. Consequently, anyone who embraces the path of peace-making becomes a child of the God of peace. Jesus's teaching in this Beatitude reveals the essence of God as nonviolent and peace-loving. In a single verse, it challenges centuries of belief in a God associated with violence and any references to a deity linked to war within the Hebrew Scriptures. This teaching dismantles any spiritual justifications for warfare.

****

Insight: This doesn't imply that there are no wars with justifiable causes. To illustrate, there exists a distinction between a conflict driven by ideology or religion and a defensive war waged against a malevolent invader who poses a direct threat to one's very existence. Early Christians wrestled with these concepts. We still should.

****

Instead, peacemaking ushers in a profound shift in our understanding of the nature of the Living God and what God's reign truly represents. Through this Beatitude, we catch a glimpse of the nonviolent essence of heaven itself, and we are invited to participate in the global endeavor to eradicate war and actively work toward the realization of a world founded on principles of nonviolence right here on Earth.

Political peace starts at the kitchen table, where families learn the transformational love of the Prince of Peace. In the time of Jesus, Pax Romana offered a deceptive form of peace by sacrificing the well-being of others for those at the top of the pyramid. The peace Jesus is talking about is Pax Christi, the peace of Christ that surpasses the false trappings of power, prestige, and possessions.

"Pax Romana," which translates from Latin to "Roman Peace," refers to a long period of relative peace and stability across the Roman Empire. This era lasted approximately from 27 B.C. to A.D. 180, beginning with the reign of Emperor Augustus (the first Roman emperor) and generally considered to end with the death of Emperor Marcus Aurelius.

Pax Romana was a peace enforced by the empire through military strength and governance. Pax Christi is a peace that emerges from the transformation of hearts and societies according to the principles of love, justice, and the teachings of Jesus. Pax Romana was temporal and limited to the Roman Empire, whereas Pax Christi is a universal vision that seeks an enduring peace for all humanity, emphasizing spiritual renewal and reconciliation.

"Pax Christi," or "Peace of Christ," represents a radically different concept of peace rooted in the teachings of Jesus Christ. It is not merely the absence of conflict but a vision of comprehensive well-being, justice, and reconciliation among people and God. Pax Christi is grounded in the values of the kingdom of God, emphasizing love, forgiveness, and service to others, especially the marginalized and oppressed.

****

Radical Attitude

Becoming peacemakers, as taught by Jesus, is a radical attitude we adopt following Jesus. His teachings emphasize the importance of pursuing peace, resolving conflicts, and promoting reconciliation. Here are some key teachings and passages from the New Testament that guide Christians in becoming peacemakers:

- **The Beatitudes (Matthew 5:9):** Jesus said, "Blessed are the peacemakers, for they shall be called the children of God." This Beatitude underscores the special blessing upon those who actively work to bring about peace and reconciliation.
- **Turning the Other Cheek (Matthew 5:38-42):** In this passage, Jesus encourages non-retaliation and responding to hostility with love and forgiveness. By not seeking revenge, we contribute to de-escalating conflicts.
- **Loving Your Enemies (Matthew 5:43-48):** Jesus challenges us to love our enemies and pray for those who persecute us. This love can help break the cycle of hostility and pave the way for peace.
- **Reconciliation (Matthew 18:15-17):** Jesus provides a framework for resolving conflicts within the community of believers. He encourages going to a brother who has offended you to seek reconciliation and peace.
- **Forgiveness (Matthew 6:14-15):** In the Lord's Prayer, Jesus emphasizes the importance of forgiving others if we expect to be forgiven. Forgiveness is a key element of peacemaking.
- **The Parable of the Good Samaritan (Luke 10:25-37):** This parable illustrates the importance of showing mercy and compassion to others, even those from different backgrounds or groups. It promotes the idea that our neighbors are not limited by geography or ethnicity.
- **Seeking Reconciliation Before Worship (Matthew 5:23-24):** Jesus teaches that if you are offering your gift at the altar and remember that your brother has something against you, leave your gift there and first be reconciled to your brother. This underscores the priority of reconciling relationships.

- **Paul's Teaching on Peace (Romans 12:18):** The apostle Paul echoes Jesus's teachings by advising, *"If possible, so far as it depends on you, live peaceably with all."* This verse emphasizes the individual's responsibility to pursue peace actively.
- **Paul's Exhortation to Unity (Ephesians 4:3):** Paul encourages believers to maintain the unity of the Spirit in the bond of peace. Unity and peace are closely intertwined, and working toward unity contributes to peace within the Christian community.

Becoming a peacemaker, according to the teachings of Jesus, involves actively pursuing peace, reconciliation, forgiveness, and love in our interactions with others. It requires a commitment to non-retaliation, the resolution of conflicts, and the promotion of harmony within our communities and beyond.

****

Beatitude Code: In the image of God, we are His children.

Lectio Divina: *"Do nothing out of selfish ambition or vain conceit. Rather, in humility, value others above yourselves, not looking to your own interest, but each of you to the interest of others."* Philippians 2:3-4 (NIV)

Chapter Fifteen

BEYOND THE BRAND

"There is one body and one Spirit, just as you were called to one hope when you were called; one Lord, one faith, one baptism; one God and Father of all, who is over all and through all and in all."
Ephesians 4:4-6 (NIV)

Everything Jesus

There are many brands of Christianity. In the Catholic tradition, you might belong to a Franciscan, Jesuit, Carmelite, Dominican, or Carmelite order. If you are Protestant, you might be Lutheran, Methodist, Anglican, Methodist, Baptist, Presbyterian, Pentecostal, Independent, or some other name. Each brand of Christianity embodies a revelation of the Holy Spirit, helping the Christians in each of its churches live "The Way." The unique virtues embodied in each brand of the Church reveal their charism, a Greek word meaning "gift."

On the road to Damascus, Paul's religious pedigree was radically transformed. He went from seeing the world in black and white to seeing the world in vivid colors. He went from seeing God as one on the judgment seat to seeing God as three persons in a perpetual dance with each other, celebrating each other. He went from seeing Jesus as human to seeing Jesus as both Divine and human, not either/or. Paul's mystical experience transforms him from being a prosecutor and a murderer of Christians to the man responsible for spreading Christianity to the civilized world. He goes from sinner to saint and remains both.

The paradox continues for each of us as we come to grips with opposing ideas, such as weakness and strength, flesh and spirit, law and grace, saved and unsaved, faith and works, and all the great contradictions we must eventually come to grips with. I have been fortunate because my parents helped me at an early age develop an open mind that allowed me to see the mysteries of "The Way." But it is Christ alone who opens my heart (body, soul, and spirit) and provides the enlightenment of my salvation.

Once, I attended a home Bible study in college as a guest of older women who all sang in the Spirit simultaneously. This was new to me. They were of a different brand of Christianity that I had never been exposed to. The ladies ended the Bible study by singing in the Spirit. Each one sang something entirely different, but the sound was what I could only imagine as angels singing in heaven. It was beautiful, peaceful, energetic, edifying, and pure. The presence of God was magnified. I never went back, nor have I experienced this anywhere else. It was a one-time event where a mystery was shared with me, one that still reminds me of the awe and wonder of God. These women shared their gifts with me. I was blessed and still am.

In my faith experience, I have been comfortable worshipping in a Catholic church with kneeling benches, incense, and chants. I have been comfortable worshipping with a praise band, lifting my arms to heaven, and dancing in the Spirit. I have been comfortable in traditional services, quoting the Apostle's Creed, singing hymns, and experiencing the Spirit of God on a pew. I've been blessed to attend churches in Africa out in the bush with half-naked people jumping up and down, praising God, and giving their all-in worship.

Ultimately, your experiences through various forms of worship invite a deeper reflection on the enormity and inclusivity of God's kingdom. It challenges believers to look beyond their traditions and comfort zones, recognizing that God is not confined to any one expression of worship. Instead, God is actively at work in all aspects of His kingdom, inviting us to experience and contribute to its richness.

This understanding calls Christians to a broader perspective of faith, encouraging a spirit of unity, openness, and curiosity about the myriad ways God reveals Himself to His people. It's a call to embrace the freedom to worship and experience God's vastness, encouraging a faith that is ever-growing, inclusive, and reflective of the kingdom's diversity.

Otherness

In Western Christianity, educated people who inherited the enlightenment and reformation tend to see things as either/or, sometimes called dualistic thinking. It often makes us take sides and divides us into combative camps rather than dynamic forces showing the world the love of Christ. Paul faced the tradition of the Jews, wanting to conserve the past, while the educated elite, the Greeks, sought to change everything. Scripture says of Jesus, *"The true light that gives light to everyone was coming into the world"* (John 1:9 NIV).

Jesus embraced otherness. Born a Jew, Jesus saw the goodness of the Roman Centurion, Gentiles like Syrophoenician women, tax collectors, eunuchs, Pagan astrologers, and zealots—sinners of all stripes His inherited brand of religion looked down on. Jesus brings us an inclusive worldview that stands in solidarity with humanity, not beyond it or above It. The radical message of the cross is a message of forgiveness and love over judgment. Still, we are prone to seek ways to divide ourselves and fall back into old patterns. Yes, we are special, and so is everything and everyone God created. I think the point of being Christian is to embrace people, love people, and leave room for God. Jesus has no problem with otherness, nor should we.

Jesus thinks beyond our ways of reasoning. He understands us better than we understand ourselves. He also teaches us to see our own nature. Jesus said, "You have heard that it was said to the people long ago, 'You shall not murder and anyone who murders will be subject to judgment.' *But I tell you that anyone angry with a brother or sister will be subject to judgment"* (Matt. 5:21-22 NIV). Socrates said to know yourself. Jesus shows us the best way to know yourself is by knowing God. God sends Jesus so we can know God.

Non-Dualism

Jesus of Nazareth can be understood as a non-dual teacher, although this perspective is not often emphasized within traditional Christian theology. Non-dualism emphasizes the interconnectedness of all existence and the oneness of God, creation, and humanity. Let's make this clear: Non-dualism does not dismiss the carnage of sin and biological truth, nor does it deny the reality of God's absolutes, physically, morally, or spiritually.

The significance of non-dualism becomes apparent when we seek a deeper understanding of Jesus's radical message. However, it's crucial to remember that Jesus came to bridge the chasm that sin had created between humanity and God. His mission is to restore us to being children of God.

Navigating the intricate patchwork of contradictions inherent in the human experience and emerging from life with a pure heart, humility, a sense of spiritual poverty, mercy, and a commitment to peacemaking is a formidable challenge. Yet it is a challenge made possible by adopting the mindset of Christ with the Holy Spirit in constant communion with our spirit. In this way, non-dualism provides a lens through which we can better comprehend the profound message of Jesus while recognizing the transformative power of enjoying the enlightenment of our salvation.

Oneness

Central to Jesus's teaching was a direct and intimate relationship with God. He often referred to God as "Abba" or "Father." Non-dualism sees the divide in the human condition as caused by sin, not otherness.

By following Jesus and receiving His Holy Spirit, we are united in a fallen world with God Almighty. Jesus was both God and human, not either-or but both. There is no separation when we choose to follow Jesus.

Love and Compassion

Jesus's teachings consistently stressed love and compassion for all, including one's enemies. He challenged the notion of dualistic thinking by urging His followers to love unconditionally, irrespective of differences or conflicts. This emphasis on universal love underscores the interconnectedness and non-dual nature of humanity, as everyone is deserving of love and compassion, created in the image of God.

Kingdom of God

Jesus frequently spoke about the "kingdom of God" or the "kingdom of heaven." Instead of envisioning this as a distant, separate realm, His teachings implied that the kingdom of God was both present and accessible within the hearts of individuals. Jesus asserts that the Divine is immanent and can be experienced within the here and now, not only in eternity. Not either/or, both.

"I Am" Sayings

In several instances, Jesus used the phrase "I am" to describe Himself, such as, *"I am the way, the truth, and the life"* (John 14:6). These declarations point to a deeper understanding of identity that transcends the dualistic ego. "I am" signifies an awareness of oneness with the Yahweh.

Humans often view themselves in terms of binary opposites, believing we either walk in the Spirit or we do not. However, the reality is more complex as we embody both states simultaneously.

Even when we reach a stage that some refer to as "sanctification," where we no longer commit sins intentionally, we remain sinful beings who are redeemed by grace. Thus, our existence is characterized by a blend of both conditions, rather than a simple either/or dichotomy.

Healing and Miracles

Jesus's acts of healing and miracles often emphasized the immediate connection between the spiritual and physical realms. These actions demonstrated that He saw no separation between the two and suggested that Divine power flowed effortlessly through Him. The incarnation is non-dual because it defies our understanding of time and space and how God works in the physical and spiritual, the seen and unseen worlds we live in.

Jesus

Recognizing Jesus as a non-dual teacher offers a fresh perspective on His teachings, emphasizing the profound unity that underlies all existence and encouraging us to embrace a spirituality that transcends dualistic thinking. It helps us see how we often limit our thinking to conditioning rather than opening our minds to Christ.

Consider this scenario: When you attend a church service, it's common to hear a sermon about tithing your finances. But have you ever encountered a sermon about tithing your time? Imagine dedicating two hours and forty minutes daily to God's kingdom work. It's worth noting that every individual possesses the same twenty-four hours in a day.

Now, ponder the potential impact if every Christian tithed their time. How might such a collective commitment transform the world and advance the cause of God's kingdom, justice, and peace?

I've discussed extensively the interconnected components of our souls (the body, mind, and spirit). Following Jesus is a journey marked by perpetual transformation, a lifelong process of continuous self-discovery and growth. The Beatitude journey emphasizes the blessings of the means itself, and in itself, the means bring the ends to be experienced in the here and now.

One of the most profound aspects of this transformation is the ability to perceive God's presence even in the faces of those we may consider our adversaries and to extend forgiveness to them. It signifies a liberation of the spirit, a higher state of spiritual consciousness.

While I've made considerable progress on the Beatitude road, I realize I have a long way to go. And yet, one of the biggest lessons I have learned so far is this: The destination takes care of itself. My responsibility is to get up each day and take the journey into the mind and heart of Jesus. That is God's will.

New Monastic Movement

Shane Claiborne, a leader in the new monastic movement for helping the poor, spoke at Emory Theological School. My brother in Christ, Jeff White, and I attended. Shane had worked early in his life in India with Mother Teresa. That alone is unique because Shane is Protestant. People serving a greater purpose, like Shane and Mother Teresa, serve a living Christ, not a brand.

Shane said each day that all those who worked with Mother Teresa would wake up hours before dawn and spend hours in prayer and worship, preparing for the day. When they left the comforts of the Abby, they went into the streets of Calcutta as the hands and feet of Christ. That is where Shane began to understand his purpose, how to serve God by serving others.

After Shane's speech during a Q&A, one of the resident theologians asked a question about the homosexual issues the church faced. The way the question was asked, it felt like a trap. Shane, with long hair, dreadlocks, and all, embraced the question with grace. He smiled and said with the glow of love, "Brothers and sisters, why do we focus on the things that divide us when we can all agree on the good of chastity?" The room went dead silent. I felt like I was in the presence of Jesus.

I have been discussing a pure heart and being a peacemaker. Shane embodied both. His Philadelphia Project revitalized old churches and buildings into living quarters for poor people. They had to be married if they wanted to live together, be responsible by holding down any form of work, and attend a daily Bible study to receive free rent. Shane had seen the face of God in the streets of Calcutta. Shane said the best way to understand a Moslem was to go to the park and pick up trash on Saturdays with them. Shane was not a talking head; he was an activist for Christ. Shane did not concentrate on what divides us, and polarization is everywhere. Shane saw Christ, who unites us.

Everyone's journey to purpose is unique and different. Just as there are no two snowflakes alike, God created each of us unique, and in the image of God. Each of us has a pilgrimage—the life we were given, our circumstances, our physical and mental being, and even our geography. We are shaped by the happenstance of our parents, our culture, and the church we grew up in or not. Followers of Jesus are used wherever they are. You are exactly where you are supposed to be because that is where you are, "just as I am."

The Beatitudes help you see beyond your brand's boundaries to experience and learn from Jesus. Once you press into the transcendent nature of faith, the Holy Spirit will help you be a light to your chosen brand. We are each called to bring the enlightenment of Christ alive for others, to love one another, be a witness to one another, to comfort one another, to suffer with one another, and so on. There are fifty-nine references to "one another's" in Scripture. It's part of living in "the Way." It is the attitude of Beatitude, being there for one another.

Jesus teaches us the Beatitudes to reveal the mysteries God hides from those who do not choose the blessings of faith. Many doors open when we choose the journey of faith. Jesus did not come and say to me, "Become like Moses." Jesus comes and says to me, "Be J. Steve

Bruner." The Beatitudes serve as a mirror, revealing my authentic self. My spirit is either alive or dead in Christ. If it is alive, this enables me to perceive the world with the vision and compassion of Jesus. Jesus didn't come to make us more spiritual per se; Jesus came to make us more human. Why? Because that is how God created us! After all, we are body, mind, and spirit – and being spiritual is part of being authentically human. It's not either or, it's both.

****

Beatitude Code: You cannot have truth without love. Truth without love is not truth. You cannot have love without truth. Love without truth is not love.

Lectio Divina: *"Enter through the narrow gate. For wide is the gate and broad is the road that leads to destruction, and many enter through it. But small is the gate and narrow the road that leads to life, and only a few find it. Watch out for false prophets. They come to you in sheep's clothing, but inwardly they are ferocious wolves. By their fruit, you will recognize them. Do people pick grapes from thornbushes, or figs from thistles? Likewise, every good tree bears good fruit, but a bad tree bears bad fruit. A good tree cannot bear bad fruit, and a bad tree cannot bear good fruit. Every tree that does not bear good fruit is cut down and thrown into the fire. Thus, by their fruit, you will recognize them. "Not everyone who says to me, 'Lord, Lord,' will enter the kingdom of heaven, but only the one who does the will of my Father who is in heaven. Many will say to me on that day, 'Lord, Lord, did we not prophesy in your name and in your name drive out demons and, in your name, perform many miracles?' Then I will tell them plainly, 'I never knew you. Away from me, you evildoers!"*
Matthew 7:13-23 (NIV)

Chapter Sixteen

THE OTHER SIDE OF THE MOUNTAIN

"Lord, I want all of you to have all of me."
Linda Heinze, a good friend

Blessed are Those Who are Persecuted for Me

Two of the most authentic figures in modern history are Mahatma Gandhi, and Martin Luther King Jr. Civil rights were led by the late Dr. Martin Luther King Jr. He modeled the movement after Mahatma Gandhi's non-violent protest in India. Gandhi led a historic movement to gain India's freedom from British rule. In the 1960s, Blacks protested in the streets of America, where racism had weaved itself deep into the fabric of American life and was viewed as someone else's problem.

Civil rights participants were committed to the highest principles of Christian beliefs and non-violent protest. In 1965, America watched Blacks being beaten senseless on a bridge in Selma on their TVs, not resisting while others prayed. The civil rights protesters were demanding justice and dedicated to non-violence, even as they faced physical harm, including bruises, broken bones, and, in some cases, death. They embodied the teachings of the Jesus they had listened to in church, demonstrating their willingness to endure suffering for the kingdom of God on earth as in heaven.

Martin Luther King Jr.'s message was a cry for justice: "I dream of the day when men will be judged by the content of their character, not the color of their skin." They lived out the Christian message, and the nation was changed. Mahatma Gandhi said about Christianity, "First, I would suggest that all Christians and missionaries begin to live more like Jesus Christ. Second, practice it without adulterating it or toning it down. Third, emphasize love and make it your working force, for love is central in Christianity."

Gandhi went on to explain the essence of how he saw Christianity: "The Gospel will be more powerful when practiced than preached. A rose does not need to preach. It simply spreads its fragrance. The fragrance is its sermon ... the fragrance of religious and spiritual life is much finer and subtler than that of the rose." Gandhi had a very close connection with Christianity and admired Jesus, often quoting from his favorite passage, the 'Sermon on the Mount' (Matt. 5-7) where the Beatitudes are found.

When the missionary E. Stanley Jones met with Gandhi, he asked him, "Mr. Gandhi, though you quote the words of Christ often, why is that you appear to so adamantly reject becoming his follower?" Gandhi replied, "Oh, I don't reject Christ. I love Christ. It's just that so many of you Christians are so unlike Christ. If Christians would really live according to the teachings of Christ, as found in the Bible, all of India would be Christian today."[15]

Both Gandhi and Martin Luther King Jr. fought tirelessly for justice. Unfortunately, their dedication to justice made them targets for those who opposed their messages. Gandhi was assassinated in 1948, while King was shot by a sniper in 1968.

Both Gandhi and King believed in the power of love and nonviolence, and they dedicated their lives to spreading this message. Their deaths were tragic, but they left a lasting impact on the world. I have studied both men. They are my heroes, men who lived with full devotion to a higher purpose, knowing the cost. Can you imagine spending the night in jail with Dr. Martin Luther King Jr., asking him how his faith gave him the courage to face all that he faced?

The Other Side of the Mountain

King's journey was not an easy one. He faced tremendous opposition from those who opposed his message of equality and justice. He was subjected to violent attacks, imprisonment, and threats to his life. Despite these challenges, King remained committed to his cause and continued to fight for what he believed in.

One of King's most famous speeches is his "I've Been to the Mountaintop" speech, which he delivered on April 3, 1968, the day before his assassination. In this speech, King spoke about his mortality and belief that he had seen the other side of the mountain, meaning he had a sense of the future and what was to come. He spoke about his confidence that the Civil Rights Movement would triumph despite its challenges and setbacks.[16]

Non-violence teaches us two wrongs do not make a right. Ultimately, choosing the path of non-violence prevails over evil, injustice, and wrongdoing. It requires a higher power and faith.

King's legacy has left us with a beacon of hope and boundless inspiration. Through his unwavering resolve, he demonstrated that we could rise above and champion justice in adversity. He illuminated the path to a better world, teaching us that no challenge is insurmountable when met with courage and unwavering faith. King's profound impact reminds us that even in the darkest times, we can overcome evil and do the right thing. His legacy continues to ignite the flames of Beatitude within us.

Who Am I? This or Another?

Dietrich Bonhoeffer is a Christian martyr who was hung on April 9, 1945 at the age of thirty-nine only days before the Americans liberated the POW camp where the Nazis imprisoned him. In college, I read a poem he wrote just before his execution. His words touched something deep inside me, as though I was looking into a mirror. Sometimes, we all wrestle with our identity and who we are because we face real-life tests and have genuine feelings. At times, we feel like we are children of God, but at other times, God may seem far away.

Most of us will not face a life-or-death test, but we all will face death eventually, and equally, we all share in the deaths of people we love. How we approach death says a lot about how we approach life.

Have you ever thought about what heaven will be like? It's a hard concept to wrap your mind around. I love skiing, playing golf, riding motorcycles, and backpacking. If heaven is better, it's safe to assume I can't imagine how good that will be. Brennan Manning, author of *The Ragamuffin Gospel* and *Abba's Child*, said he thinks when we get to heaven, Jesus will ask us one question: "Did you believe I loved you?"[17]

I had a dream, and in that dream, heaven was like a Parisian five-star hotel and restaurant, people coming and going, busy streets outside, inside were tall ceilings, so tall, and people were flying kites inside. Everyone was engaged in deep conversation, laughing, celebrating, and listening to each other, hanging on to every word the other person said.

You were free to be who you were. You were you, nothing less, nothing more. It was total satisfaction. No one had anything but time, the clothes you wore, and no worries or possessions. Everybody shared everything freely. You did not have to prove yourself. Just be yourself. There was acceptance everywhere, no judgment, overwhelming love of life and each other. There were strangers everywhere, and you knew you had eternity to get to know them, every one of them. In God's kingdom, everyone is equally important, and everyone is wrapped in this love and acceptance. There was no rush, no anxiety, and more places to go, but no need to rush, just being in the moment. Everything was happening as it was supposed to.

In those moments before a martyr dies, I think they experience the kingdom of heaven because they already live in the kingdom of God, the present reality of God's power and glory. That is the path the Beatitudes prepare us to live out in our daily lives.

Jesus goes to the cross, beaten, humiliated, and without bitterness, and says, *"Father, forgive them for they know not what they do"* (Luke 23:24). To face death, as we all will, requires the courage of faith. When God is present as promised, one sees beyond the veil, beyond the pain, beyond the loss, and into infinity.

The Cost of Discipleship

Dietrich Bonhoeffer wrote the poem "Who Am I?" while he was imprisoned, reflecting his deep theological and existential contemplations only weeks before his death by hanging. It poignantly explores the contrast between how one is seen by others versus one's perception of self, particularly in the context of suffering and the facade one might present to the outside world. This poem, like much of Bonhoeffer's writings from his imprisonment, is a profound meditation on identity, faith, and the nature of God's presence amid suffering. The following is my favorite section:

Who am I? This or the Other?
Am I one person today and tomorrow another?
Am I both at once? A hypocrite before others,
And before myself a contemptible woebegone weakling?
Or is something within me still like a beaten army,
Fleeing in disorder from victory already achieved?
Who am I? They mock me, these lonely questions of mine.
Whoever I am, Thou knowest, O God, I am thine![18]

The poem goes to the core of our identity, our humanity, and the choices we face daily to live the life we were born to live. We always have the choice to be less or to be more in Christ. Bonhoeffer reminds us of the questions of life "Mock me," but he concludes the poem with, "Whoever I am, Thou knowest, O God, I am thine." That is the Beatitudes wrapped into a well-lived life, not a straight line, but one that navigates the contours of a satisfied soul. In Dietrich Bonhoeffer's final moments, he may have quoted, "Even though I walk through the valley of the shadow of death, I fear no evil, for You are with me."

Dietrick Bonhoeffer was "poor in spirit." He knew how to mourn. He had a pure heart. He saw God. He hungered and thirsted for righteousness. He stood for justice in the face of Nazi hell. He tried to be a peacemaker and would not succumb to evil. He, like Jesus, did not want to die but was willing to put God's will first.

Bonhoeffer was an accomplished German intellectual, theologian, and pastor. His faith experience was far ahead of his time. His diversity took him to America to study theology, and while there, he taught Sunday school at a Black church in Harlem. This was not the typical white theologian of the 1930s. He was a founding member of the Confessing Church, which opposed the Nazi takeover. He wrote the renowned book *The Cost of Discipleship*. When World War II broke out, he was safe doing work in England. He did not have to return to Germany, but he chose to go back to stand beside the few brave Christians who opposed Nazi terrors.

Dietrich Bonhoeffer faced his doubts under the most extreme circumstances. He was able to keep the main thing the main thing, the main thing being to live into God's will. Jesus was his example. What separates Jesus from all of us is Jesus always kept the main thing the main thing. Jesus always did the will of His Father. When we do God's will (following Jesus), we see God is constantly working wonders, and with a God sense (faith), we see God at work. We do not stand to the side, indifferent; we are in God's will, participating in His kingdom work.

The faith journey encapsulated within the Beatitudes unfolds as an odyssey of profound revelations. With every stride along this sacred path, we draw nearer to the heartbeat of God, unraveling the intricate tapestry of our most authentic selves. In this enigmatic pilgrimage, we unearth the essence of blessedness, a life imbued with the fortuitous and blissful union of our innermost being, transformed and transcendent.

****

Beatitude Code: The Beatitudes are the art of living perfectly imperfect lives.

Lectio Divina: *" If I speak in the tongues of men and of angels, but have not love, I am a noisy gong or a clanging cymbal. And if I have prophetic powers, and understand all mysteries and all knowledge, and if I have all faith, so as to remove mountains, but have not love, I am nothing. If I give away all I have, and if I deliver up my body to be burned, but have not love, I gain nothing.*

Love is patient and kind; love does not envy or boast; it is not arrogant or rude. It does not insist on its own way; it is not irritable or resentful; it does not rejoice at wrongdoing, but rejoices with the truth. Love bears all things, believes all things, hopes all things, endures all things.

Love never ends. As for prophecies, they will pass away; as for tongues, they will cease; as for knowledge, it will pass away. For we know in part and we prophesy in part, but when the perfect comes, the partial will pass away. When I was a child, I spoke like a child, I thought like a child, I reasoned like a child. When I became a man, I gave up childish ways. For now we see in a mirror dimly, but then face to face. Now I know in part; then I shall know fully, even as I have been fully known.

So now faith, hope, and love abide, these three; but the greatest of these is love."

1 Corinthians 13

******

Thank you, Dad, for showing me what grace looks like.

******

THE BEATITUDE CHRONICLES

"The Beatitude Chronicles" is author J. Steve Bruner's Substack (blog) that enriches the book's wisdom with an informative and inspirational perspective.

https://stevebruner.substack.com

Explore New Horizons:

- **Reflections on Scripture**: See Scripture through the lens of the Beatitudes.
- **Celtic Christianity**: Spiritual disciplines that awaken the Beatitudes.
- **Enneagram**: How your personality type relates to the Enneagram, where to test yourself, resources, and coaching tips.
- **Beyond Dualism**: Learn to think non-dualistically like Jesus.
- **Dessert Wisdom**: Explore the wisdom of ancient contemplatives.
- **Existentialism**: The journey to know your authentic self through knowing God with lots of Kierkegaard made easy to understand.
- **Meditation**: Reasons to meditate, techniques, and journaling.
- **Reflections**: Inspirational writings inspired by the Beatitudes.
- **Community**: Meet the author and fellow seekers.

"I'm seeking to build a community of people who embrace the Beatitudes and want to share in its treasures. Let's get to know and grow with each other." J. Steve Bruner

ONLINE RESOURCES
- stevebruner.substack.com
- www.beatitudecode.com

Endnotes

1. *The Chosen*, season 2, episode 8, «Beyond Mountains,» directed by Dallas Jenkins, written by Tyler Thompson, Dallas Jenkins, and Ryan Swanson, featuring Shahar Issac, Jonathan Roumi, Elizabeth Tabish, et. al, aired July 18, 2021, Angel Studios, 2017.

2. *The Matrix*, directed by Lana and Lilly Wachowski (1999; Burbank: Warner Bros., 1999).

3. Søren Kierkegaard, *The Sickness Unto Death*, Translated by Howard V. and Edna H. Hong (Princeton: Princeton University Press, 1980).

4. Cynthia Bourgeault, *The Heart of Centering Prayer: Nondual Christianity in Theory and Practice* (Boulder: Shambhala, 2016).

5. Thorleif Boman, *Hebrew Thought Compared With Greek* (New York: W.W. Norton & Company, Inc., 1960).

6. Francis Brown, S.R. Driver, and Charles A. Briggs, *A Hebrew and English Lexicon of the Old Testament*, Edited by Edward Robinson (Oxford: Clarendon Press, 1994).

7. Estera Wieja, "Blessed in Hebrew: The Meaning Behind the Word Baruch," Fellowship of Israel Related Ministries (FIRM), April 30, 2020, Accessed February 17, 2023, https://firmisrael.org/learn/the-hebrew-meaning-of-blessed/.

8. Richard Rohr, *Eager to Love: The Alternative Way of Francis of Assisi* (Cincinnati: Franciscan Media, 2014).

9. Eckhart Tolle, *A New Earth: Awakening to Your Life's Purpose* (New York: Penguin, 2005).

10. Ibid.

11. Watchman Nee, *The Spiritual Man* (Bon Air: Christian Fellowship Publishers, 1968).

12. Albert C. Outler, *John Wesley's Sermons: An Anthology* (Nashville: Abingdon Press, 1991).

13. Rick Warren, *The Purpose Driven Life: What on Earth Am I Here For?* (Grand Rapids: Zondervan, 2002).

14. R.T. Kendall, *Total Forgiveness* (Lake Murray: Charisma House, 2012).

15. Mahatma Gandhi, *The Collected Works of Mahatma Gandhi* (Bristol: Obscure Press, 2008).

16. Martin Luther King, Jr., "The Other Side of the Mountain," Speech presented in Memphis, Tennessee, April 3, 1968.

17. Brennan Manning, *Abba's Child: The Cry for Intimate Belonging* (Colorado Springs: NavPress, 2002).

18. Dietrich Bonhoeffer, *Letters and Papers from Prison* (enlarged ed.) (Minneapolis: Fortress Press, 1997).

Acknowledgements

No book emerges in isolation. Authors and thought leaders like Søren Kierkegaard, Richard Rohr, William Barclay, Francis of Assisi, Thomas Aquinas, E. Stanley Jones, Blaise Pascal, Thomas Merton, M. Scott Peck, Louie Giglio, Rick Warren, Brennan Manning, R.T. Kendall, John Piper, Henri Nouwen, A.W. Tozer, Watchman Nee, Erwin Raphael McManus, the Desert Fathers & Mothers, and Celtic Christian writers – their works have inspired and informed me. Likewise, throughout this journey, I've been blessed with the friendships of many incredible individuals, each passionate about exploring the things of God with open minds and hearts.

To these remarkable friends, my deepest gratitude. It's also essential to acknowledge some specific people whose support has been foundational to this work. Jeff and Ann White have been friends who shared this journey with Sherry and me. Jeff's unwavering dedication and numerous hours engaging with and critiquing my ideas have been invaluable. My spiritual guide, Dick Vigneulle, was a bright light, fueling my quest for a deeper connection with God through his profound wisdom. In a heartfelt moment before his passing, I expressed regret for not spending more time with him. His reply was comforting and eternal, "Steve, we are united in our mission for the Lord. Don't worry. When we all get to heaven, we'll have eternity to catch up." Dick meant it.

Bill Johnson, depicted as the angel within these pages, was nothing short of a miraculous friend. His constant encouragement to pursue writing and showing up when my family needed his friendship & discernment was miraculous.

To Sherry, my wife, and the music of my life, enduring the erratic schedule of a writer is no small feat. Your patience and support have been the quiet force behind this endeavor. Thank you. I love you!

My father, a kindred spirit in my love for scripture, history, and philosophy, possesses an extraordinary gift of communication that has always inspired me. As for my mother, she was a force of nature—her passion unparalleled, her love boundless, and her creativity infinite. She left an indelible mark on the hearts of all fortunate enough to cross her path. It is from her, I believe, that my desire to write emerges.

To my beloved son Stephen, his awesome wife Sarah, my wonderful daughter Shelli, her amazing husband Mike, and my extraordinary grandchildren Brooks, Graham, Reese, Truett, Harper Kate, Ellie, and Winnie: I present this book as my legacy. You each have my blessings, and I am immensely proud of all of you as you continue to carry forward the light and love of Jesus.

****

"Your Word is a lamp to my feet and a light to my path." Psalms 119:105 (ESV)

****

Blessings to everyone who played a part, no matter how big or small, in bringing this book to life. Your collective wisdom, support, and love have been the guiding lights on this journey of creation. And to my readers, I hope we find ways to stay in touch with each other. Living by the Beatitude Code, we can change the world, one person at a time.

Printed in the USA
CPSIA information can be obtained
at www.ICGtesting.com
JSHW010240180624
64990JS00001B/1